SOLVING THE P

www.fieldingfinancial.com

SOLVING THE PROPERTY PUZZLE

A guide to successful property investment

Secret Millionaire

GILL FIELDING

SilverWood

Revised Edition published in 2016 by SilverWood Books

SilverWood Books Ltd
14 Small Street, Bristol, BS1 1DE, United Kingdom
www.silverwoodbooks.co.uk

ISBN 978-1-78132-537-7

British Library Cataloguing in Publication Data
A CIP catalogue record for this book is available from
the British Library.

Typesetting by SilverWood Books
Printed by Latimer Trend & Company Ltd on responsibly sourced paper

For Martin, Emma, Michael and Claudia,
without whom nothing would be possible – or worthwhile

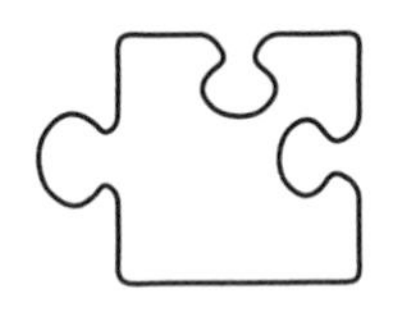

CONTENTS

Useful Information

BTL – Buy to Let

B&F – Buff and Fluff

HMO – Houses of Multiple Occupation

CP – Capital Project

FPD – Fancy Pants Deal

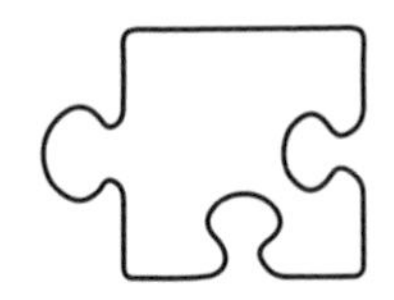

CHAPTER 1

The Foundations

Like many, I started my property investing career as an amateur landlord[1]. I had decided, at the age of eighteen, to go to university and, for some bizarre reason, I didn't understand that you could get accommodation there, so I set myself the Herculean task of buying myself a house so that I could get educated.

I worked for about fifteen months in all manner of jobs: the VAT office in Southend during the day; a leisure centre by night; I delivered leaflets during my lunch break and worked in pubs and did a cleaning job at the weekends. The money from my spare jobs meant that I was able to save almost my entire salary from the VAT office (about £4k pa) and, in July 1977, aged nineteen, I bought my first house in Burgess Hill about eight miles from the campus of the University of Sussex.

At the time, I remember a choice: buy a flat outright or push the boat out and buy a house with a small mortgage. I pushed the boat out and went for the house, which shot up in value almost overnight. It wasn't as easy as it sounds. I had wanted to buy a place

1 I'm going to use the term 'landlord' to mean landlord or landlady throughout; partly because it's easier and partly because the term landlady (although, of course, that's what I am) makes me feel like an apron-clad buxom woman controlling a Blackpool boarding house (which, of course, I am not). So, apologies if the generic, but masculine, term bothers you.

in Brighton where many other students lived, but even then, Brighton was a fashionable place to live and prices were always high. So, after visiting the university, I drove back home to London, up the A23, and passed a place called Burgess Hill where I discovered that I could buy a proper family three-bedroom house for the price of a tiny flat in Brighton, so that's exactly what I did: I bought a three-bed semi there for just under £7.5k.

I lived in it for a while but the journey to the campus felt huge and my friends were all in Brighton. So, I ended up moving into town and renting out the house. When I left university in 1980 I sold the house for nearly £30k, quadrupling my money and becoming well and truly smitten with property as a wealth-creating vehicle. I've been investing ever since.

I often think that had I had better support, knowledge and guidance as a teenager, somebody might have told me that university provided accommodation, and I might never have bought that house and caught the bug.

But maybe I would because I have always loved property: big houses, little flats, grand houses, slums – the lot. I like looking at houses, visiting the grand ones (have a look at my personal favourite: Hardwick Hall in Derbyshire), walking the streets and looking at different areas of property. So I guess I was always likely to be an investor eventually. However, my university experience forced the issue and got me into the game earlier than most. But other than that initial passion I don't think I had any particular skill that enabled me to get started. I certainly wasn't very good at the numbers then, and it was a good ten years before I could wield a calculator with any enthusiasm or accuracy. I was also a people-watcher so was fascinated by the psychology of it all, and most importantly, having done it so successfully once, nobody could tell me that I couldn't (although many tried!). So, I was off and running. And now, nearly forty years later, I'm a serial investor and the majority of my lifetime money and wealth has come from property.

According to Legal & General, property prices have risen by about 4,300% in that time and, over that period, I have invested through every up, down, peak, trough, boom, bust and panic, and I've seen every property investing fad, fancy, failure and flop come and go.

During those four decades I have continued to invest, sometimes heavily and sometimes not, and obviously I have gained masses of experience; but perhaps more importantly, what I now have is *perspective.*

Like anyone skilled and experienced in their art I can now see, and often predict, market movements ahead of time. I don't get fazed or disturbed by market falls; in fact, I quite like them, and I've seen more or less every type of market before. Consequently, I know my way around each type. When your perspective of the property market is like mine, where I see the market in terms of where it's been for forty years, and the massive growth it's gone through, then not much panics you.

On the chart, X marks the spot when I bought that first house and look at how much appreciation there has been since then – brilliant, isn't it?

House Prices in UK

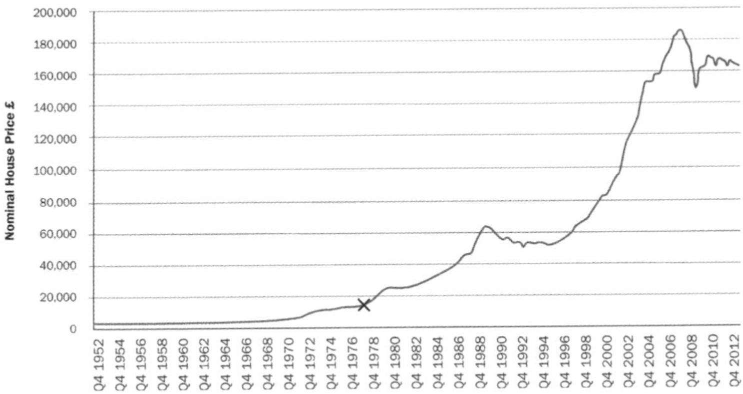

Nominal House Price £

But I'm getting ahead of myself and getting into the detail already. What I really want to share with you in this introduction is a flavour of my experience to reassure you that this book is worth reading.

So I've invested for nearly forty years so far, and I am still going, by the way!

I've invested in good old-fashioned buy-to-lets, HMOs (Houses of Multiple Occupation) and I've refurbished, renovated and developed. I've bought and sold quickly on some little ones, and some big ones, and I've kept a few. I own land, I've developed pubs, I've extended and enhanced; the only thing I've never, ever done – and I say this with enormous pride – is bought a new build property (and more, oh, much more, on that later!).

My investing has changed of course; I started with small properties and, overall, my investments have got larger. I also do a lot more joint ventures nowadays; in fact, every property I've been involved in over the last year has been a joint venture of some kind as I've needed, for personal reasons, to become a lot more hands-off than ever before. And that's the beauty of property investing, and doing it properly – it can be flexible to suit you and your personal circumstances. Again, I've invested during my single days, during motherhood (three times), during periods of serious employment and during periods of unemployment too.

The one thing that has remained constant through all those times is my desire to do this properly and professionally. From the very beginning, I was aware that this was a serious business and investing isn't a game, a part-time hobby or something you do after watching one of the vast array of TV programmes on the subject.

Incidentally, I've now done a fair bit of TV myself but I've never done a property programme, and that's because I can't get any TV company interested in showing property investing seriously – or properly. I guess it's just not entertaining enough on one level, and I do get that, but it is a shame.

Property investing is a serious and profitable business if done properly. It fulfils a social and moral gap, it's flexible and can change with you and your circumstances; and it's the only business worldwide that has a potential customer base of 100% – because everybody lives somewhere!

In summary then, property investing works – for all sides: the investor, the seller, the purchaser and the tenant, as well as for the financial services industry, finance providers and, of course, the government. I have become quite opinionated about the government's approach to housing over time – and again, more on that later.

The UK Property Education Business

I don't want to leave this introduction without explaining a bit about the growth of the property seminar business and my part in it. It's difficult to believe now that there was ever a time without some version of property investing on the TV, on the Internet and being provided somewhere in the UK, probably on a weekly basis, in the form of property education seminars, or property coaching and mentorships.

It wasn't always that way, and I invested on my own for about twenty years.

When I started, in the late 70s and throughout the 80s, property investing wasn't really talked about. There certainly weren't magazines, seminars, TV programmes or websites devoted to it like there are now. It took me twenty years to make my first million in property and my rough guess is that nowadays it takes a newcomer about two years if they invest professionally.

My excuse for taking so long is that I was alone, didn't have any guidance or education in it, and never shared my experiences or talked about my investing with anyone – in fact I don't think I even met another investor until the late 1990s. And I presume I would have been content to just continue investing privately like that for evermore, but in 1996, my life changed.

I was sitting in my kitchen one day when there was a frantic knocking on my door and I opened it to find my bank manager standing there. He and I had become quite friendly (by then I had started to accumulate serious money and bank managers tend to like that), and he occasionally popped in for a cuppa, but this day he was flustered.

I invited him in and put the kettle on while he waved a leaflet at me. He had been sent a pack of leaflets from head office with the instruction to include the new product they were promoting in his monthly sales targets. He was suddenly presented with a product he needed to understand, embrace and, most important for him, sell.

We both looked at the leaflet with trepidation and concern. The terminology was new and unfamiliar, full of legal phrases and incomprehensible. We didn't even understand the title of the product, because it was strangely called a:

BUY-TO-LET MORTGAGE

It's difficult now to look back and understand what an impact the introduction of the buy-to-let mortgage had in this arena. Of course, people like me did take out borrowings to buy properties, but they were all personal borrowings. Suddenly, in 1996, here was a product that defined what I did.

The introduction of the buy-to-let mortgage changed my life forever. It gave me credibility and endorsed what I did – it enabled me to come out of the closet in a bizarre way, because now, suddenly, it was a legally defined 'proper' activity with an identifiable name. At that time I think I believed that the only landlords out there were of the accidental variety or were landed gentry just renting out their spares; suddenly I realised that there were others like me, out there somewhere, who were doing this as a career.

And the rest is history: I quickly worked out what the bank manager's crazy product was and explained it to him, and he then referred me on to all his contacts and connections who wanted to understand what this newfangled thing was. I became an expert – well, frankly, at that stage I was just the person who knew just a little bit more than anyone else about it.

From there I started to write about it; a friend had just launched a magazine with pages that needed filling so I started writing about property, and some of the information that is well tried and tested in the property education business now came from that period of my life and the stuff that I was writing back then.

I then got asked to speak about it – just the occasional conference – and from there, I decided to present my own property investing seminars, starting those at the very end of the 1990s. They were small affairs, held only once or twice per year, normally in Brighton, or sometimes Gatwick, and the audience was always a mixture of locals out for the day, combined with a smattering of interested but uninformed investors. Until one day, when I had an American in the audience, which created quite a stir with a group of ladies from the local Women's Institute.

I approached him at the coffee break and asked him what on earth he thought he was doing. He said he was an investor in America and was in the UK on business and thought he'd pop in to see what the UK property market was like. I was, of course, completely gullible and accepted this explanation without really questioning why an American businessman should be in a seminar run for locals needing a break from walking on Brighton pier.

So I accepted his presence, but the following day I received an email from a man in America who told me that he owned a large property education business in the States and that he had planted a spy in my camp the day before, and could we meet?

We met at Gatwick shortly after and the American offered me a variety of things: tea, a blank cheque to buy my business and a job (to set up a property education business for him in the UK), all of which I refused – well, apart from the tea obviously.

But I did accept a consultancy position to write property training for him and to train some trainers, speakers and mentors, so that he could expand his business into Europe, starting with the UK. And that was it – from that inauspicious start grew the first major property education business in the UK. I ended up working with that organisation for about six years, from 2002 until 2008, both speaking for them and training their speakers and mentors, and I'm delighted to say that many of the current batch of property education businesses and speakers came from the people I trained back then.

And of course there are many property education businesses now – including my own!

For me, those small, innocuous seminars I ran in Brighton in the 1990s have now turned into a substantial and exciting property education business and we provide all the information and support anyone could need to become incredibly successful at it, so I am very grateful for all of the years of learning and graft I've had – often in solitude – because it means that I'm now in a position to help others with their journey.

I'm not saying categorically that I was the only property seminar business in the 1990s or that I was the first, but in all likelihood I was because sources of property education must have been very few and far between back then, otherwise I would have found them. Also, in the years since then, I have met and spoken to many, many thousands of people about property education and no one has ever mentioned a similar experience to mine – but if you had one, then please get in touch; we can reminisce about the old days!

Finally, I can say that property has given me immense pleasure

– and profit. I've had fun, laughed a lot, cried a little and met some amazing people. It's one of the most interesting and passionate places to have a business, and I can't recommend it highly enough.

And so I have written here, in a couple of hundred pages, what it's taken me nearly forty years to learn and experience in the hope that it guides you, motivates you and sparks you into action. This country needs more professional investors as we have a ticking time bomb of a problem with housing in this country.

Please come on in – I hope I get to meet you soon. I'm often around in the property investing circuit, so come and say hello. I'll see you there.

Reading Tips

Information changes all the time in this business so I have included, where I can, sources, references and websites, but web addresses change constantly and if a web address doesn't work for you, then don't panic. Firstly put the gist of what I'm saying into a search engine and see if you can locate the information yourself – if you still can't find it, contact our office and we will locate it for you.

Our organisation, Fielding Financial, can be found at www.fieldingfinancial.com and we report each month to our customers about the market and its changes. We have regular newsletters, webinars and seminars, so if you want to get access to any of those please contact the office at enquiries@fieldingfinancial.com. If you go on to our website you will find an area where you can download free copies of the checklists referred to in this book. You can access them directly at **www.fieldingfinancial.com/propertypuzzle**.

The Important Numbers

Inevitably we're going to be looking at a lot of numbers when we get involved with property investing, and although I'm a numbers person myself, I know a lot of people aren't so don't worry. None of the figures or calculations are that difficult and we'll take them in stages, but you do have to get to grips with some numbers, so you either need to do that yourself or get a buddy that can do it with you.

So let's start from the big numbers and work our way down.

The Population

According to the last accurate count of people taken from the Census in 2011, the population of the UK is:

63,181,775

England	53,012,456
Scotland	5,295,000
Wales	3,063,456
Northern Ireland	1,810,863

Now if we just take England, the overall population is 53,012,456 and those people live in twenty-two million properties, so on average there are two and a bit people living in each property.

Now, more importantly for us is the split of ownership, which is:

Owner occupied (65%)	14.3 million households
Privately rented (18%)	4.0 million households
Socially rented (17%)[2]	3.7 million households

The reason I include this batch of figures as our first number is this: it gives us a sense of the overall demand for our product.

2 Includes 'council' and housing associations.

Property investing, if done properly, is a serious business and I wouldn't start any business at all without identifying my demand – and here we have it: the total potential demand for what I'm doing (if I just stick to England) is about fifty-three million – because everybody lives somewhere (with very few exceptions).

Imagine that: a business with 100% demand for the product!

Property Investors

How many property investors are there?

Well, when I first started in 1977 the answer must have been 'a few', and even in 1996, when the buy-to-let mortgage was introduced, we have no idea really because we weren't an identified force at the time; but buy-to-let lender Paragon have estimated that it can't have been more than a few tens of thousands, so let's say fifty thousand to be generous.

There were about twenty million housing units then. The majority – about two thirds – were owner occupied and the remainder were housing units provided by the state, local authorities or councils. Therefore, the proportion of properties or housing units supplied by private investors must only have been a percentage or two at best.

But had you been investing in 1996 the returns would have been enormous, and research suggests that a buy-to-let property has returned 16.3% per year, year in and year out, from 1996 to 2014. That compares to returns from share investments at 6.8% per year and interest from savings in the bank at an average of 4% over the same period. (Source: Paragon Mortgages.)

Just think about that for a moment! What that means is that for every £1k invested in buy-to-lets in 1996, you would have made £12k profit – now that's not bad for a bunch of crazy weirdos and outcasts, which property investors were back then.

But things have changed dramatically in the last twenty years, and property investing and property investors have now gained ground and numbers, so let's go to the property investing present.

The Property Present

Of course nowadays we have every statistic, fact and figure about all investors and what they get up to.

So I can tell you that there are now approximately two million property investors and their average age is fifty-six.

They now own 4.9 million properties, worth, estimates say, a total of about £1,000 billion – give or take a few quid. So that works out at about an average of £200k per property.

Approximately 18% of all homes or accommodation units are now owned by private investors – that's almost one in every five properties, and an increase from the 17% we saw in the 2011 Census. And of course that 18% figure is hugely significant because it is now higher than properties provided by the state or local authorities.

That's quite impressive. And of course these figures and proportions for private investors will only get bigger and bigger over time, particularly as the government are keen to help us.

They are keen to help us because they have got themselves stuck and cannot now provide housing as they used to. In 1980, one in three properties were provided by the state, but now it's only 17% and that figures drops every day, partly due to the Right to Buy legislation brought in by Margaret Thatcher in 1980. Since then, over two million council homes have been sold.

Now that two million figure equates almost exactly to the number of people currently registered on the Local Housing Authority waiting lists.

Of course, at the same time as the reduction in state-provided accommodation, we have had the reduction in the number of people who own their own homes. That figure is down to approximately 64% and is expected to drop to only 49% by the year 2032.

With the number of people owning their own homes falling at the same time as the number of state-provided houses, we as property investors have to step in and mind that increasing gap.

The opportunity is this:

- If owner-occupied households are 49%, and

- 'Social housing' provision is 17% or less

- The 'gap' between the two is expanding, meaning that the number of privately rented properties has to grow in the next eighteen years from 18% today to a whopping 34%.

And that's why the government should like us investors: because we do an important job for them and provide housing where they can't.

Their encouragement often goes unnoticed by the world at large, but there are two significant pieces of evidence to suggest that they are on our side.

Firstly, in April 2000, mortgage interest tax relief was finally abolished for residential mortgages but not for buy-to-let or investment mortgages. Up until then we used to get tax relief on all mortgage payments, including those loans taken out to buy our own home. So now only property investors get that tax relief. (For the time being anyway – see 2016 Postscript.)

And then in April 2014, the mortgage affordability rules or the MMR (Mortgage Market Review) came into play for people applying for residential mortgages, where they have to declare all their spending, even gym membership and haircuts, as part of their mortgage application. But once again buy-to-let investors have been excluded from this, and so no affordability criteria apply to us – resulting in cases now where ordinary residential buyers are *pretending* to be buy-to-let investors so that they can get loans. How the world has changed there, then.

So property investors have been encouraged by the government in the past, and part of me thinks that the current pensions changes, where we can take all of our pension money out and spend it or invest it ourselves, is another piece of government encouragement for property investors.

After all, the timing is perfect – the average property investor is fifty-six and the age you can draw these private pensions is fifty-five.

The Property Market and Take A RIDE

So, now we know the total demand for our product and who we are as a group of people, where do we start to analyse the property market?

Well, again I always start at the top and look at the market overall and then work my way down to an individual property, and I have developed a set of criteria to do that, which I have crammed into a mnemonic called **A RIDE** (I use mnemonics a lot as a memory aid because I have the attention span of a gnat and I need them to keep me focused).

I call the following analysis of the market '**Take A RIDE**'.

Now what **Take A RIDE** does is highlight the five areas that impact the property market on an international, national, regional and even individual street level.

What Is 'Take A RIDE'?

Take A RIDE is the way that I remember the areas to review before I start investing any money anywhere. It forces me to get a bit of perspective and research, and evaluate the bigger – or macroeconomic – position. It stands for:

A Actual evidence.

R Ratio.

I Interest rates and borrowings.

D Demand and supply.

E Economy and employment.

In detail, then, what are we looking at?

ACTUAL EVIDENCE

Now the past is no guarantee of the future and we have to be wary here, but we need to get evidence of what is happening to the property market before we leap in as it might give us some indications of where it might go in the future.

But let's be careful about what evidence we take, because most people in the UK have an opinion about property prices, even if it's just about their own home. But in all honesty, there's not much in the way of informed opinion about and you need to learn to sift through that, ignoring most of it, and rely on research that is more accurate and solid.

So in general, feel free to ignore:

- Your neighbours.
- Your colleagues at work.

- The taxi driver (these are very vocal 'experts').
- Your mate up the pub/gym.
- The red-topped newspapers, as they love a shocking property headline. The national obsession in the UK is about property prices, so it's always used as a good headline lead to encourage people to buy the paper.

I say 'in general' because it might just be that your mate/taxi driver/neighbour *is* a property expert – but if they claim they are, ask for their evidence. Can they show you any? How long have they been doing it? Have they been successful? What's their evidence of success – number of properties, an amount of profit, or what?

For instance, when I present property seminars I always show the attendees photos, figures for several of my investments, the associated legal documents and correspondence as well as copies of my bank statements and my credit report.

So many people consider themselves to be property experts when they don't own anything other than their own home (which isn't the same!), so be careful of accepting false claims.

Evidence We Can Accept

The principle is to look for independent third-party evidence where possible, and the more independent and the more qualified the better, so consider:

- Any organisation that has no vested interest: the government, the Bank of England, the Council of Mortgage Lenders (CML).

- Any related body: the Land Registry (but their data can be a little out of date in comparison to some) and HMRC.

- Trade organisations: the Royal Institute of Chartered Surveyors (RICS), and those individual surveyors who are members of RICS.

- Some websites, including:

  - www.checkmyarea.com
  - www.wizzamania.com
  - www.zoopla.co.uk
  - www.rightmove.com
  - www.mouseprice.com

- Research from either educational establishments or, in the main, financial lenders, although with the latter always check what they are saying and why they might be saying it, just in case there's a promotional element to it. Even then, the underlying numbers might be OK, but always check the source of the data.

- Some of the more serious newspapers such as *The Times, Sunday Times* and the *Telegraph*.

In Summary

The best evidence we can find is authenticated and from an independent, qualified third party. The more evidence and the longer the trend, the better.

What Are We Looking For With Evidence?

What we are looking for is trends and some evidence that the area we are looking at is in line with – or contrary to – the market overall.

We can also see how the prices in a specific area are already being affected by external events – or whether that effect is yet to come – and make some decisions about strategy and location.

Just to illustrate, I am going to take an article from the *Telegraph* at the very end of 2014 and show you how I would read it and the action I would take. It is reporting on the annual price statistics report published by the Nationwide. They are reputable sources for me.

The Telegraph, Wednesday 31st December 2014

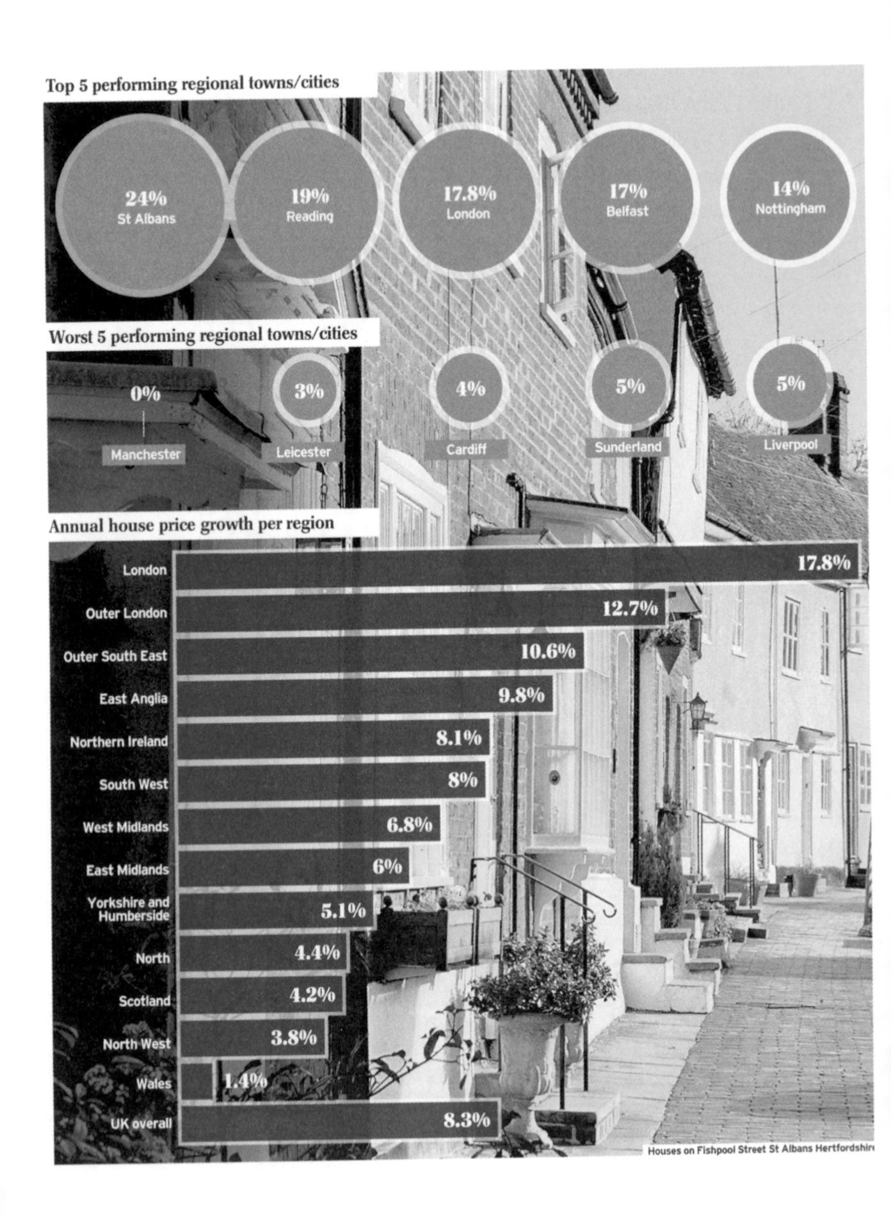

Houses on Fishpool Street St Albans Hertfordshire

Now the things that I immediately pick up in reading these articles are:

- Manchester. Now, Manchester was our top performing price-rise city in 2013, when the published price rise was 20% over the year, and now for 2014 it's the worst performing city at 0%! I would immediately go and look at Manchester to check all the other parts of Take A RIDE to see if it has overcorrected and is in line for a mini surge.

- I would try and work out why Reading and St Albans had done so well, and I can save us all time here and say it's to do with railways: London Crossrail is being extended out to Reading, while the north-south tranche of that is going north of London. Now that makes logical sense to me and I can probably conclude that those areas have had their big uplift and ignore them for the short term.

- I can start to highlight areas I will look to for potential investment, and what I do there is:

  - Ignore anything that had a big uplift in 2014, as it is unlikely that it will be a top performer in 2015. Look for longer-term trends by comparing against prior years to see if an area is on a slow but relentless move up.

  - Take the average movement for 2013 – the 8.3% – and then delve deeper into those areas which *underperformed* that figure last year. I would check if there was any other evidence to suggest that it might underperform, or perhaps more likely overperform, the average in the following year.

So that highlights for me the potential areas that all increased less than 8.3%, which are:

- Northern Ireland
- South West
- West Midlands
- East Midlands
- Yorkshire and Humberside
- North
- Scotland
- North West
- Wales

NB: now before you get carried away and immediately go and invest in those places, please DON'T!

There are other reasons why I wouldn't touch some of these areas with a barge pole – it's just a start before I whittle down where I would look to invest.

Once I have my few areas to look at from this quick scan I can then look at the other parts of Take A RIDE to see what else might direct me to an investment area.

Decent evidence is the property investor's friend. It can direct you to potential areas of investment, explain market movement and warn you where to avoid at all costs, but it takes perspective and experience to read evidence well, so the quicker you start practising that, the better!

RATIO

This ratio is otherwise known as the affordability ratio, and it is a specific property-based thing as the ratio shows us the affordability of housing at the moment for the property market as a whole, as well as regionally and locally.

The premise is that the more affordable houses are, the more people will be able to buy, so the demand for houses goes up and, as long as supply doesn't change much, then prices have to rise.

So a ratio that favours affordability is likely to suggest that prices are about to rise.

You find this by calculating the house prices as a proportion of people's individual earnings. So if the average house price is £150,000 and the average earnings are £25,000 then the ratio is simply 6, because 25 goes into 150 six times.

In order to see why this is so useful as a measure we need to look at the extremes. If the average house price stays at £150,000, when average salaries go up to £50,000 we can immediately see that the ratio has fallen to three:

Imagine how we feel at this point – we earn £50k, we can afford to buy our own house so we dive into the property market, creating demand, and the more people that go into the property market, the higher prices will go.

Let's look at the reverse, and now our salary is £15,000. We can instantly see that the ratio has risen to ten: £150k/£15k. **Oh no!** Imagine what that does to the market, because nobody can afford to buy at these prices when their salaries are so low, so demand leaves the marketplace and prices fall.

Overall then, we can see that if the ratio is high, and ten would certainly be very high, then property prices are likely to be going down.

Conversely, if the ratio is low, and three would be low, then property prices would most likely be going up.

We now have a guide: three is low (prices should go *up*), ten is high (prices should come *down*), and I can tell you that the middle range, over time, is about 4.5–5.5.

How Can I Use This Information?

There are two main ways I use this:

- It gives me a sense of where the overall market is going, and I can then decide whether to go into this particular investment or not (it helps with our analysis of **Actual Evidence**).

- I can then compare a local area with the overall average and see if one specific local area is lagging behind the country as a whole. If I find one – and that's simply finding an area where the ratio is lower than the national average – I have a good idea that the specific area I am looking at is likely to come up in value more quickly than the average. And that's the area where I want to invest!

- I can get very specific with this and actually calculate ratios for individual towns (by using the local government housing and salary statistics), and even individual streets if I want to.

This gives me a really strong sense of the direction of the market overall, and it also provides a measure of long-term perspective.

Let's look at some specifics (and if you're not a numbers person take a deep breath now, because the next chart could be quite scary).

If you want to download the data in full yourself then: click on the data area of the Nationwide bank website: www.nationwide.co.uk/about/house-price-index/headlines. Then you should see a sub-menu, and you click on the 'Download data' button. At the bottom of that page you will see 'Affordability Estimates', and then choose 'First Time Buyer House Price Earnings Ratios'.

Then you can download the spreadsheet that gives you the quarterly indices or ratio from 1983 to date, by area. The UK average is the far right-hand column and the specific areas are the other columns.

NB: the Nationwide does have some housing data going back to 1952, so if you're interested in longer-term trends, look around their downloads area; that's as good a place to start as any.

Why Use the First-Time Buyer Ratio?

I use the first-time buyer ratio because that is the most sensitive to any current market conditions as properties are, on average, the cheapest and therefore reflect movements more significantly. If the first-time buyer market is moving, then the rest of the market will automatically follow as people move up the property ladder.

First Time Buyer Gross House Price to Earnings Ratio

First time buyer gross house price to earnings ratios

Source: Nationwide

	Northern	Yorks & H	North West	East Mids	West Mids	East Anglia	Outer SE	Outer Met	London	South West	Wales	Scotland	N Ireland	UK
2007 Q1	4.3	4.6	4.5	4.7	5.0	5.2	5.6	5.6	6.8	6.0	5.1	3.9	7.1	5.1
2007 Q2	4.4	4.6	4.6	4.8	5.0	5.2	5.7	5.8	6.9	6.0	5.2	4.2	7.7	5.4
2007 Q3	4.2	4.6	4.5	4.7	4.9	5.2	5.8	5.7	7.2	6.1	5.1	4.1	8.1	5.4
2007 Q4	4.3	4.6	4.4	4.6	4.9	5.2	5.7	5.7	7.1	6.0	5.0	4.1	7.6	5.4
2008 Q1	4.2	4.5	4.4	4.6	4.8	5.0	5.5	5.5	6.9	5.7	4.9	4.0	6.6	5.2
2008 Q2	4.0	4.2	4.1	4.2	4.6	4.7	5.2	5.2	6.5	5.5	4.6	3.9	5.7	4.9
2008 Q3	3.8	4.0	4.0	4.1	4.4	4.4	4.9	4.9	6.3	5.1	4.4	3.7	5.4	4.7
2008 Q4	3.6	3.7	3.7	3.8	4.1	4.2	4.6	4.6	5.8	4.9	4.2	3.6	4.9	4.4
2009 Q1	3.1	3.4	3.5	3.4	3.9	3.8	4.3	4.4	5.4	4.7	3.5	3.4	4.8	4.1
2009 Q2	3.2	3.6	3.5	3.6	3.9	4.0	4.5	4.6	5.7	4.7	4.0	3.5	4.1	4.2
2009 Q3	3.4	3.6	3.6	3.7	3.9	4.2	4.6	4.8	6.0	4.9	4.0	3.5	4.5	4.4
2009 Q4	3.3	3.7	3.6	3.8	4.0	4.3	4.7	4.8	6.1	5.0	4.0	3.5	4.4	4.4
2010 Q1	3.3	3.7	3.6	3.9	4.0	4.2	4.8	4.9	6.2	5.0	4.2	3.5	3.9	4.4
2010 Q2	3.3	4.0	3.8	3.9	4.2	4.3	4.9	5.1	6.5	5.3	4.1	3.7	3.6	4.6
2010 Q3	3.3	3.7	3.6	4.0	4.3	4.3	4.8	5.1	6.4	5.2	4.1	3.5	3.8	4.5
2010 Q4	3.4	3.6	3.7	3.9	4.0	4.3	4.7	4.9	6.2	4.9	3.9	3.3	4.0	4.4
2011 Q1	3.2	3.7	3.7	3.8	4.0	4.2	4.7	4.9	6.2	4.9	3.9	3.3	3.6	4.4
2011 Q2	3.0	3.6	3.7	3.8	4.1	4.4	4.7	5.1	6.5	5.2	4.1	3.4	3.7	4.4
2011 Q3	3.3	3.6	3.6	3.9	4.1	4.4	4.8	5.2	6.4	5.2	3.9	3.5	3.6	4.5
2011 Q4	3.3	3.6	3.6	4.0	4.1	4.4	4.7	5.1	6.5	5.0	4.0	3.4	3.5	4.4
2012 Q1	3.3	3.5	3.6	3.9	4.0	4.3	4.8	5.0	6.4	4.9	3.8	3.3	3.4	4.4
2012 Q2	3.2	3.5	3.5	4.0	4.1	4.2	4.8	5.1	6.7	5.0	3.8	3.3	3.0	4.4
2012 Q3	3.2	3.6	3.5	3.8	4.1	4.2	4.7	5.0	6.6	5.0	3.8	3.2	3.0	4.4
2012 Q4	3.1	3.4	3.5	3.9	4.0	4.2	4.7	5.0	6.6	4.9	3.8	3.2	3.1	4.3
2013 Q1	3.2	3.5	3.5	3.9	4.0	4.2	4.7	5.1	6.7	5.0	3.9	3.1	3.2	4.3
2013 Q2	3.2	3.5	3.5	3.9	4.1	4.4	4.8	5.2	7.1	5.0	3.8	3.2	3.3	4.4
2013 Q3	3.2	3.6	3.6	4.0	4.2	4.5	4.9	5.3	7.3	5.1	4.0	3.2	3.3	4.5
2013 Q4	3.2	3.7	3.6	4.1	4.2	4.5	5.1	5.5	7.6	5.3	4.0	3.3	3.4	4.6
2014 Q1	3.2	3.7	3.7	4.2	4.3	4.8	5.2	5.6	8.1	5.4	4.0	3.3	3.4	4.8
2014 Q2	3.4	3.7	3.8	4.3	4.3	4.8	5.4	6.1	8.9	5.6	4.2	3.4	3.7	5.0
2014 Q3	3.3	3.7	3.8	4.4	4.5	5.0	5.5	6.1	8.9	5.6	4.1	3.5	3.7	5.0
2014 Q4	3.4	3.7	3.7	4.3	4.5	4.9	5.6	6.2	9.1	5.7	4.0	3.5	3.8	5.0
2015 Q1	3.5	3.6	3.7	4.3	4.4	5.0	5.5	6.3	9.1	5.6	3.9	3.4	3.8	5.0
2015 Q2	3.4	3.7	3.7	4.4	4.5	5.1	5.7	6.5	9.5	5.7	4.1	3.4	4.0	5.1
2015 Q3	3.4	3.7	3.7	4.4	4.5	5.0	5.8	6.7	9.7	5.9	4.1	3.3	3.9	5.1
2015 Q4	3.5	3.7	3.7	4.3	4.5	5.1	5.9	6.8	10.1	5.8	4.0	3.3	3.9	5.2
2016 Q1	3.4	3.7	3.7	4.4	4.5	5.2	5.9	7.1	10.1	5.8	4.0	3.3	3.7	5.2
2016 Q2	3.4	3.7	3.8	4.4	4.7	5.3	6.1	7.2	10.4	6.1	4.0	3.3	3.8	5.3
2016 Q3	3.5	3.8	3.9	4.5	4.7	5.4	6.1	7.2	10.3	6.0	4.1	3.4	3.9	5.4

1. Long-Term, National Trends

If we look at the far right column (the UK) for a moment, and quickly glance down the numbers shown, you will see the ratio starts at 5.4 in Quarter 4 of 2007, the last time that property prices peaked in the UK, and then gradually drops to 4.1 by Quarter 1 of 2009, when the market fell.

Then it waves about between 4.1 and 4.5 between 2009 and the beginning of 2013, when our property market stagnated, and then, starting in Quarter 2 of 2013 up until the end of 2014, it has gradually risen to 5.0 as our property market has picked up again. Now we're more or less back where we started at the start of 2008.

Now, if we monitor this ratio regularly, and we get estimates of this monthly, we can start to get a sense of trends, peaks and troughs with a more solid piece of evidence, rather than the 'guesstimates' we find elsewhere.

2. Regional, Comparative Trends

If we keep the UK average for the end of 2014 in mind and then look along the bottom row of figures, which show the regional ratios for that period, they vary from 3.4 in the North to 9.0 in London!

Well, that's no surprise is it? We know from all our other evidence that London prices are ridiculously high and, in all honesty, London is such a big market that this average ratio doesn't mean much and could be distorted by a few of the massive houses in Central London.

So for London ignore the big ratio and find more local ones yourself.

But if you look at the regional ratios, the ratios that are below the UK average of 5.0 are:

The North	3.4
Scotland	3.5
Yorkshire	3.7
North West	3.7
Northern Ireland	3.9
Wales	4.0
East Midlands	4.3
West Midlands	4.5

This indicates that these areas have the greatest capacity to move up more quickly than the average because they are more affordable than the average, and what people do is to buy houses in the cheaper areas where they can afford to live.

The caveat to the above is that those people probably also need to get a job, hence we look at employment together with these figures – and this is included in **Take A RIDE under E**.

Now go back to our list above – does it look familiar? It should do, as it has picked up exactly the same areas we identified in the review of the housing statistics in the Actual Evidence section above, which were:

- Northern Ireland
- South West
- West Midlands
- East Midlands
- Yorkshire and Humberside

- North
- Scotland
- North West
- Wales

Aha!

Summary of the Ratio

What the ratio does is endorse the Actual Evidence analysis. On the one hand, that's not a surprise because the house prices themselves form one part of the ratio calculation, but on the other, we have added on to it the employment and affordability criteria, which gives another dimension, and another level of accuracy and credibility, to the data.

The ratio reflects the property market and its trends.

The long-term average is slightly under five and if the ratio is lower than that then prices are likely to start moving up; higher than that and prices are likely to be heading down.

The more extreme the difference from five, the more significant the movement is going to be.

Invest with confidence if the ratio falls below that overall figure, and look at investing in areas where the local ratio is *lower* than the national figure.

Experienced Investor's Tip

Looking at the two things we know so far, then, the Actual Evidence and the ratio, it's looking like our next investment should be up north, and we should start looking for opportunities there – but be careful, we've still got a long way to go and a lot more information to gather first!

INTEREST RATES AND BORROWINGS

Unless you are going to make your investment purely for cash (and that's probably a bad idea anyway), the rate of interest that you pay is vital as it's the largest cost in your property investing business. Most interest rates are derived in some way from the national bank rate – in the UK this is the Bank of England base rate, and all other interest rates are usually somehow connected to that main headline rate – so keep an eye on the headline rates at all times.

If you are really keen you can monitor the Bank of England's Monetary Policy Committee (MPC) in the UK to see what they are taking into account when making decisions about the interest rates, and this may give you a head start in applying for funding. For instance, there are nine members of the MPC and if they are all voting for the interest rates to stay the same there's less pressure for change, but if they vote 5–4 to stay the same you can tell that there's more chance that rates will change in the near future.I personally keep a very close eye on this, and I report on it in my newsletters.

This macroeconomic view gives you a steer on where interest rates are going to go and then you can decide how to fund your property investing business. Although there are other criteria to consider, if you are a cautious person, or don't like to take on risk, then you are much more likely to fix the interest rates on your borrowings and for as long a period as possible.

MPC

The MPC was formed in 1997 and it was one of the first things Gordon Brown, as the then Labour Chancellor, did when they got elected that year. Up until then interest rates had been firmly guided by the government of the day and consequently could fluctuate wildly based on political activity. Just imagine: an election looms so interest rates go down; the government get re-elected; interest rates go up! The formation of the MPC removed much of the political bias and provided some much-needed accountability and independence. The MPC consists of nine people from a selection of academics, government officials and external bodies and organisations, each having one vote. They are chaired by the Governor of the Bank of England.

Look on the Bank of England website (www.bankofengland.co.uk) for the identities of the current MPC and to get access to their decisions, minutes of meetings and action taken.

One result of the formation of the MPC is that interest rates don't fluctuate like they used to. See the chart!

Economy Tracker: Interest Rates Since 1694

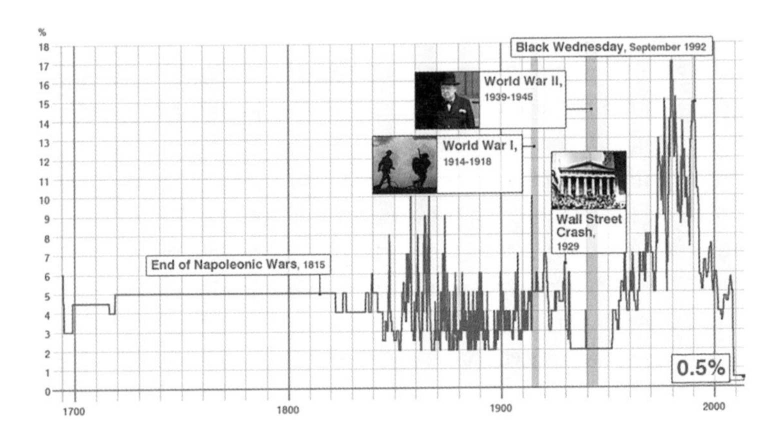

At the time of writing, the base rate in the UK had been 0.5% for about six years, and has now dropped to 0.25% and that's unprecedented since records began in 1694. That's a very stable rate and time period, and one of the consequences of that is that lenders are much happier to lend on fixed rates for long periods of time. At the moment, you can get a ten-year fixed-rate deal certainly for under 5% per year (and probably a bit less), and a five-year fixed-rate deal for just under 2% per year.

NB: please ask your financial advisor for current rates.

Those figures are extraordinary and have never been so low in this country's history.

Then what happens is that when uncertainty starts to creep into the interest rates, and a change in rate looks imminent, the finance providers stop these long-term low rates and will only fix lending for shorter periods of time, and usually at higher rates.

Fixed Versus Variable Rates

There is no one answer as to whether you should take out fixed or variable borrowings for your property investing, and both have advantages.

If you fix for long periods you have more certainty in your profit and cash flow, and perhaps you may sleep easier at night if you are of a nervous disposition. The disadvantage of fixing is that it can be costly if you change your mind, as there will normally be redemption penalties if you repay the loan early (ERCs). Now, as property investors you need flexibility to sell a property if you get a good offer, or if the market changes or you change your strategy. If you do that you then need to calculate the cost of redemption and add that into the financial assessment of the situation you're looking at.

Variable borrowing, on the other hand, tends to be slightly cheaper overall and is more flexible for movement and change in circumstances, but it carries with it a degree of uncertainty, although that's difficult to say when interest rates have just been static for six years!

Overall though, and over the long term, using variable rates for your borrowing will work out slightly cheaper than fixed. This is because when offering the fixed rate, lenders always add a bit to the rate they charge as a contingency and insurance to cover their risk, just in case the base rate moves against them in the period of the fix.

Finally, my experience is this: when people start off this investing business they are more likely to fix and when they get more experienced and get a bigger portfolio they tend to go variable – but it's up to you!

Good Debt Versus Bad Debt

We hear and read a lot about the difference between good debt and bad debt, and my view is that borrowing for any consumer spending on stuff like sparkly shoes and fancy cars is bad debt.

However, borrowing for investment may be good debt as long as it passes two important tests:

- Does the investment you are looking at generate enough money to pay all of the interest charges, either on a regular monthly basis (income strategies) or as a lump sum at the end (capital strategies)? Be careful with capital strategies as you may go broke while you're doing the project, because the second and more important test for good debt versus bad is:

- **Cash flow**! No debt is ever good debt if you go broke paying it. So, for instance, if your investment is estimated to produce a 10% return on your money and the borrowing is only 5% then it looks like good debt, but if the return only comes once – say, at the end of a twelve-month project – but the interest payments are monthly, where are you going to get the money for those regular interest payments?

So, if you are going to do capital-type projects where cash doesn't come in monthly, your overall projects need to include a fund or a contingency measure to cover the interest.

NB: this is probably the most compelling reason why novice investors should NOT do capital projects at the beginning!

Interest Rate Summary and Other Considerations

Fundamentally, the lower the interest rates, the more demand there will be for borrowings and, specifically in the property market, the lower the interest rate is, the higher the demand for property gets, and usually the higher property prices go.

Now I say *usually* because we have to look at two things together in the property market: the rate of interest (which at the time of writing is very low, and a good thing) in conjunction with the availability and rate of borrowings and financial products.

When the financial market is tight the number of products available from the finance lenders restricts and, as investors, we have little or no choices there, but when the economy is bright and stable then the number of products increases and we have more choice.

During the credit crunch period (2008–2013) the number of mortgage products available was very low, but from the middle of 2014 onwards the products have been increasing at an amazing rate and we are currently seeing new product options being released every week.

Mortgage Transactions

In addition to the above, and despite the rate of interest being low, if no one will lend money then that suppresses all demand and keeps property prices low.

As a rule of thumb, there needs to be about one hundred thousand mortgages per month in order for the mortgage market to be in full 'flow', and to be reacting to the requirements of the marketplace. This includes both new mortgages and remortgages. You can get these figures from the media section of the CML at www.cml.org.uk.

The number of mortgages being issued is affected by:

- The rates on offer.
- The availability of suitable products.
- The lenders' willingness to lend.

As a final comment on this section I have to say that all of the changes in mortgage affordability criteria we have seen since early 2014 will have suppressed the property market to some degree.

DEMAND AND SUPPLY

Then we have the old demand and supply issue. In the UK we are still – by the government's admission – short by about 250,000 housing units each year, and while demand constantly outstrips supply, the market price must rise. So, when I look at the economic fundamentals I can see that there is still strong support for the housing market – low interest rates and high demand.

We know that the market has been struggling with a huge imbalance, inadequate supply versus high demand, which has been partly held at bay by the lack of funds available for purchase; but eventually that will move and you can keep up to date with the figures via information published by the RICS, reports from estate agents and websites, which will all show changes in activity.

Look at specific demand and supply statements from the government in the housing and household section of www.gov.uk/government/statistics.

The Supply Versus Demand Imbalance

There have been a variety of government departments and ministers from Kate Barker onwards who have looked at this inequity of supply and demand – I think even John Prescott had a go at this one – and they have all failed to make a difference.

They have failed through no fault of their own. I'm not into political backbiting but the problem is a huge one and one that needs a huge solution, which no government can afford to take, either financially or politically.

We currently have demand for at least twenty-two million homes in England, and it is an increasing figure broadly because:

- We have an expanding population (only just, and our ageing population adds more to that each year rather new births). This also leads to demand for a different type of housing.
- Socially our family profile is changing, where more and more

people live alone or in small units rather than the larger family units. The divorce rates also contribute to this one, where demand suddenly jumps 100% from one home to two.

- Net migrant inflows, where we have more people coming into the country than going out.

At the same time we have a shortage of supply of accommodation and, specifically, the right type of accommodation.

Estimates vary as to how short our shortfall is; generally, it is quoted as 250,000 units needed per year for about twenty years to catch up.

That's basically impossible to do, partly because we just don't have the workforce to build that many. As a consequence, our shortfall gets bigger each year and now we need to build another city the size of Birmingham to get anywhere near what we need.

Theoretically it is possible because, surprisingly, we do have the land and we have built on a very small proportion of the UK at the moment – estimates are that we have only built on about 8–10% of our land, and that an additional 1% of our land's resources would be enough to clear the problem.

However, there are significant governmental issues, both at a national and local level, that stop that release of land.

There is also the effect of 'land banking' by building companies, who hold the land, waiting for a more profitable time to build or sell. And that's without pressures from all the local populace having their say, which normally equates to NIMBY (Not In My Back Yard).

It's a huge problem that can only be solved by a huge solution, and everything we are currently doing is only nibbling at the corners. We need swathes of housing at a time when approximately one-third of all our housing is built painstakingly slowly, one house at a time, in gardens of existing properties.

Big Solutions Needed

The last time we had a desperate housing shortage one of our national tactics was to build garden cities – Milton Keynes, for example – and we're at it again. We have a plan to build three new garden cities, with the first two being named as Bicester and Ebbsfleet.

It's a good start – but it is only a start to what needs to be a massive house-building government policy. These new garden cities are expected to have fifteen thousand new homes in each, so even if we do build all three, that's a total of forty-five thousand homes – or just 2% of the current local authority housing waiting lists.

We need more. In fact, estimates by the Future Spaces Foundation suggest that we need a total of *sixty-seven* new garden cities, each with *thirty thousand* homes, just to cope with the shortage in London and the south east.

So while I applaud the three that we're getting, and I don't want to be churlish when it is a positive step, it's like trying to empty a swimming pool with a teaspoon.

UK Housing History

We have some interesting things to learn from our country's history here, and the only time we *have* built houses at an appropriate rate was in the couple of decades after the end of the Second World War.

That was partly because of the destruction caused by all of the bombing, partly because we had all the men returning from war wanting to go to work and providing the labour force, and partly because the respective governments of the day made it a priority.

Here's an excerpt, with a few amendments, of an article from *Conservative Home*:

> Housing is the first of the social services. It is also one of the keys to increased productivity. Work, family life, health and education are all undermined by overcrowded homes. Therefore a Conservative and Unionist Government will give housing a priority second only to national defence. Our target remains 300,000 houses a year. There should be no reduction in the number of houses and flats built to let but more freedom must be given to the private builder. In a property-owning democracy, the more people who own their homes the better.

Harold Macmillan was made housing minister, even though he claimed to know nothing about the subject. He treated it as a 'war job' and ensured that sufficient land and materials were directed towards the manifesto pledge. He also changed the name of the Ministry of Local Government and Planning to the Ministry of Housing and Local Government, to reflect the priority that housing now took.

By 1954, less than ten years after the end of the war, housing production in the UK peaked at 354,130, of which 239,580 were council houses and only 92,420 private.

The following Labour government did better: the Labour manifesto for the 1964 election said this about housing – a pledge of sorts:

> Labour will also increase the building of new houses, both for rent and for sale. While we regard 400,000 houses as a reasonable target, we do not intend to have an election auction on housing figures.

In fact, Harold Wilson's government built 425,830 homes in 1968, of which 184,450 were council and a staggering 226,070 private. The remaining houses built were typically, institutional builds, self-builds and other non-standard residential property.

Private house-builders have never since exceeded this 1968 figure. For the whole of the post-war period, despite upturns and downturns in the housing market, they have averaged 154,000 a year in the UK, and this will never be enough on its own to meet our housing needs.

House Building, House Prices and Economic Growth

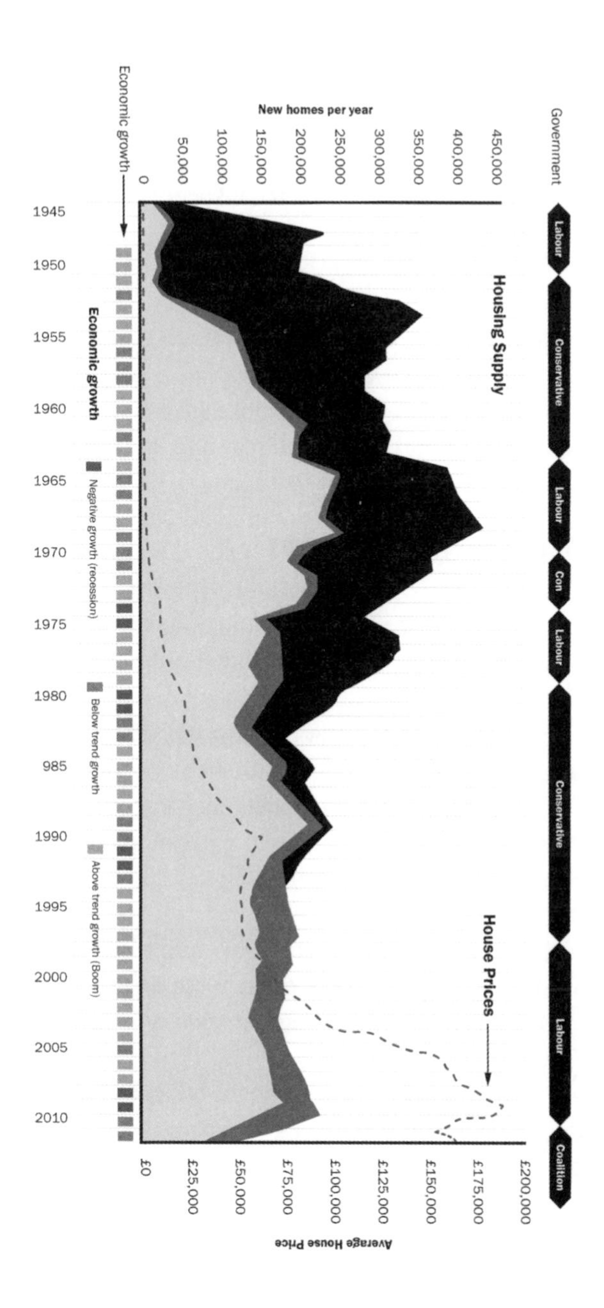

Local Demand

We have looked here only at national demand and the big picture but, of course, it's the local demand that's important for any specific property investment, so make sure that you find out all you can about that. The best place to start is the local council's Unitary Development Plan (UDP) or business plan, which will also provide you with lots of other useful information about the area, such as development proposals and communications links.

To get any area's UDP go to: www.[the area you want to look at].gov.uk.

If you're not a web person, go along to the council offices and ask, and they should be able to show you a copy of their UDP and then, most likely, sell you one. It looks like a series of telephone directories, can be quite copious and may also include development proposal maps.

ECONOMY AND EMPLOYMENT

We have already touched on some of the parts of our national economy that impact property prices. The overall economy, or macroeconomy, also impacts property values by:

- Creating confidence for individuals to buy, if the economy is strong. All that stuff we hear on the news about growth in our GDP (Gross Domestic Product) encourages us to have confidence and that transfers into a desire to buy stuff – including property.

- If the UK economy is doing better than, say, other European economies then some people come to the UK to get employment and, consequently, demand for housing increases.

- The UK property market is seen as the overseas investor's haven, and the UK government's decision to encourage, or at least not discourage that view, just fuels property prices, in London specifically.

The Government

I'm not deliberately government-bashing here, nor do I care which political party is in or out – they're all just as good or as bad as each other – but I do wish that people with experience and knowledge of all sides of the housing crisis could get a chance to have some input here, rather than people who are not interested in long-term solutions, just in solutions that will help them to win an election in five years' time.

If anyone is genuinely interested in that you can contact me via the website noted at the back of this book.

Employment Levels

Employment levels are the final piece of our assessment jigsaw. When we have high employment levels then property prices in particular will rise, because when people have jobs, they buy houses, demand goes up, and, while supply is limited, then prices have to rise.

So the employment – or more usually the unemployment – statistics are key. To give you some sense of measure, consider this:

- The lowest that this unemployment figure can be is about 1.5 million. At that level most economists would say that was more or less 'full' employment as there would always be approximately that number of people either between jobs or permanently unemployed.

- The highest that this has been in recent history is during the very high unemployment times of the early 1990s, when unemployment reached in excess of three million.

Take A RIDE Summary

My guess is you didn't expect that kind of heavyweight section so early in a book about starting property investing, but it's important for two reasons:

- I hope it highlights how seriously professional investors take this business, and to what detail we go to research our marketplace.

- It's important to see which big economic factors have an impact on smaller ones, like the price of a specific property at the end of your street.

Once you've got to grips with **Take A RIDE**, you'll soon start to apply it to your local area because you can evaluate **Take A RIDE** for a specific town or individual street or even part of a street. Sometimes getting the evidence is tricky at a very local level (you may have to read a lot of local newspapers to get a sense of the local employment situation, for instance).

No one part of **Take A RIDE** is more important than another. So I *can't* tell you that if interest rates hit 2.6% then prices will start to drop; I *can't* say that when the ratio gets to 5.43 in the North then the market will turn and I *can't* tell you what will happen to the market overall if our GDP goes above 3%.

But what I *can* tell you is that if you monitor these criteria over time, and if you monitor these five economic issues together and regularly, you will start to get a sense of how the property market moves and how the macroeconomic environment is affecting you and your personal investment choices.

Take A RIDE has to be used as an investing tool and as a guide to collate and assess evidence. The more layers you have, and the more cumulative the evidence, the more you can rely on it for your investing decisions.

Action Plan

CHAPTER 2

Money Matters

Over the years, I have had many people come up to me and say proudly, "I own three properties and I've bought them all for cash!" Then my heart sinks and I think to myself, 'doughnut', and I know I'm in for a difficult conversation. This person is clearly an amateur, and what they express with pride is the most stupid thing a property investor can do.

Now I have to say clearly at this stage that most people don't really understand property investing, and many newcomers don't get the difference between buying their own home (where buying for cash is great) and buying for investment (where it's a silly thing to do).

Unfortunately, many generations of mothers have told us that borrowing is bad and that belief has now become stuck in our collective DNA, but we have to get over it, otherwise our investing is limited.

As a mother myself, I have to make the distinction very clear: **borrowing for consumerism – borrowing to buy shoes or a car or a computer game or whatever the latest craze may be – is bad**!

But borrowing to invest is good – as long as you learn the principles. So, principles, here we come!

There are four main money matters that concern an investor:

- Value.
- Return.
- Cash flow.

- Yield (but you'll soon find out that I don't care all that much for yield).

Let's start with the biggie, then:

Property Values

The talk at all polite dinner parties is always about property values because it's an exciting topic in the main, and for most people their home 'earns' more than they do while working for a living. Imagine that! You slog all day for forty-odd years to find that your residential property actually generated a bigger slug of money for your retirement than your salary ever could.

And that's because property prices in the UK seem to be on a more or less relentless upward march, and that's been true for all of our recorded history.

Warning!

Although property prices do go up relentlessly, they don't go up in a straight line. If you look at any graph showing property prices, you will see the line wobbling about. Do you remember the song 'Jelly on a Plate'? Well it's like the song says: 'Wibble, wobble, wibble, wobble'. Property values go up a bit, down a bit and sideways a bit; but overall, and over the long term, they go up.

The big question is: how much do they go up?

There are several answers to that, depending on where you start and the research you look at, but overall we can all agree that they go up – a lot.

There is evidence to show that 10.2% is the running average, and that comes from the Domesday Book analysis.

Now the Domesday Book was written between 1066 (Norman Conquests) and about 1089, and it was a record of all significant events: births, marriages, deaths and property transactions. All of these things are still recorded, but in different places, and the property part eventually became the Land Registry. Interestingly, in the UK we have some kind of record of all property transactions since 1066 to date – eat your heart out, America!

Eventually of course, some smartypants person at a university somewhere decided to put all these figures into a computer and work out a running average price movement for property based on transactions completed and came up with the magic number of 10.2% per year, from 1066 to date, not far off a thousand years of history.

So for longevity that statistic gets the prize, but not for accuracy.

When you look at the details underlying that research we find that the notes in the Domesday Book weren't always helpful, so a property could be transacted for £100, a bale of hay and a goat, so not always an amount that we could translate into today's financial terms. However, it's a start and an estimate we can put on the list.

One of the problems we have with this long-term evidence and assessment is the lack of interest in property investing in the past, and it's only since property investing got interesting, from, say, the late 1990s, that we have any real solid facts or statistics at all.

So let's go back there. We know that in 1996, when the buy-to-let mortgage was introduced, there were only a handful of investors, but we also know that those handful of investors did pretty well.

Paragon Mortgages, one of the largest lenders in this arena, tell us that a typical buy-to-let property bought in 1996 would have increased in value by 16.3% between 1996 and the end of 2014.

That's a whopping return, and over the same period has outperformed anything else – deposits, bonds or shares – and is likely to be a more accurate return than the Domesday Book analysis.

I could continue to provide evidence and research and statistics, all showing slightly different rates of growth in value from this date to that date, but actually it isn't that important because there are four important things to note:

- Property values in the UK go up *a lot* over time.
- They go up faster at certain times than others, and sometimes go down. They also increase at different rates depending on the geographical area, type of property and time of year.
- What matters more for professional investors is finding the property that is more likely to go up, and at a faster rate than any average running at the time.
- And the most vital part:

You learn how to do that – so education is key.

Returns

In simple terms there is no point in making an effort if you don't know how much you're going to get from that effort – so calculating, knowing and understanding the return on your time and money is important.

In the last couple of pages, we have looked broadly at a certain return, the increase in property value or the growth in the capital value.

We can express that as a percentage – say, 10.2% or 16.3% – and understand that as a rate of return for our money. In fact, that headline figure is often quoted in our national newspapers, on the TV news and on the Internet. But be careful as those headline averages may contain some distortion or weighting in how they are calculated. Note them by all means, but get used to calculating the specific return for *you* on all properties *you're* interested in. Nothing matters to you more than *your* money in *your* pocket.

Capital Growth

So the first return, then, is the capital growth. You discover this by taking the current price or value, which may be just an estimate or a rough guess at this stage. You then deduct the original price or value to create an overall gain, which you then divide by the original price to get a percentage increase.

Here's an example:

> You estimate that the current value of your property is £140,000 and you bought it for £80,000 five years ago
> Calculate £140,000 – £80,000 = £60,000
> Then to get the percentage:
> Calculate £60,000/£80,000 x 100 = 75%

75%, then, is the return we have made from this property in five years, and if we wanted to be clever we could just divide that figure by five to get an annual growth figure – approximately 15% per year.

(Now I say 'approximately' there because the mathematical purists amongst us – myself included – know that the growth isn't linear and we haven't taken account of growth on original growth or the compounding effect, but jeepers, we've got to start somewhere!)

Return On Cash Invested (ROCI)

Now am I allowed to say at this stage that this is my most favourite calculation of all time? It is definitely my favourite child; I know I'm biased but let me prove to you how great this calculation is.

In fact it is really the only calculation that matters; as I've mentioned already, what we care about is *our* money: *our* returns on it, not averages or estimates.

Let's start by taking the last example on capital growth, which we now know is 75%. We can dig deeper and let's say the property was bought with a 75% Loan to Value (forever now referred to as LTV) mortgage.

Doing a simple calculation, we now know that there was a £60,000 mortgage, i.e. 75% of the purchase price of £80,000.

If you struggle with that, all you need to do is:

Calculate £60,000/£80,000 x 100 = 75%
Or, to work it back from the 75%:
Calculate 75/100 x £80,000 = £60,000

NB: it's a coincidence that both the gain and the mortgage are £60k at this stage

Therefore, if we purchased this property with a 75% LTV mortgage then our input to the purchase must have been £20,000 and, if we do all of the calculations again, we can see that the return on our cash invested (remember the magic ROCI) is:

£60,000 (the total gain) / £20,000 (our input) x 100 = 300%

And finally, if we divide that by the five years we have owned the property, our annual growth rate is:

★ 300%/5 = 60% ★

60% is quite different from the 15% we first calculated – so which would you prefer?

I'm assuming you said the 60% – but if you didn't please go and seek medical attention immediately.

And of course the reason it jumps up to 60% is that you – as the owner of this property – are getting the gain on the **whole** of the property value, not just your bit, which tends to be the deposit.

The £60,000 mortgage is just a loan, it doesn't care about growth; all the mortgage provider cares about is getting their money back, so you have no obligation to pass on any of the gain in property value to them, and your gain has become larger just because you borrowed money.

And because this is so important to your future property investing life, I'm going to do this calculation again on the assumption you had not a 75% LTV mortgage, but an 80% LTV mortgage.

The gain is still the same at £60,000 but your investment is not the £20,000 as before, but now only £16,000.

Proof:

The mortgage amount is:

80/100 x £80,000 = £64,000

Purchase price of £80,000, less the mortgage of £64,000, leaves £16,000 for us to contribute to this property

Our gain then changes to:

£60,000/£16,000 x 100 = 375%

Our gain has now increased from 300% to 375% just because we took out a bigger mortgage, and if we bought this property with an 85% LTV mortgage our gain would go up to:

£60,000/£12,000 x 100 = 500%

A 90% LTV mortgage would give you a gain on your money of:

£60,000/£8,000 x 100 = 750%

A 95% LTV mortgage would give you a gain of:

£60,000/£4,000 x 100 = 1,500%

And if it were possible to borrow 100% of the money, the return on your cash – which is nil – would be **infinite**.

At this stage you may have your mum's voice in your ear saying, "Don't borrow money," and you are going to have to learn to ignore that inner voice and go with the numbers here for the moment.

The fundamental principle is this:

The more you borrow, the higher the return on your money will be.

And read that sentence as many times as you need to, to 'get it'.

But in order to quieten your mum's (or any negative) voice, I will cover the mortgage repayment issue in a few pages' time. Jump to that section now if you, or your mum, are hyperventilating.

At this stage, I am going to quit while I'm ahead and just cover the **ROCI** on the principle or capital part of the property, but I will return to it again in much more detail in the next chapter on income properties, as it becomes even more amazing then.

Cash Flow

A property that you live in doesn't generate any cash *in* flow, it just generates cash *out* flow in the form of the mortgage payments, or maybe the rent, so on your normal home or residence this isn't a relevant number or calculation at all. However, it becomes hugely important when you are investing.

And that's because of this:

If the property doesn't produce a positive in flow of cash, either on a monthly basis with the rent or in the form of a lump sum on a property that you are refurbishing/doing up, then you're not doing this right.

There is *no* circumstance in which it is right to take on a property that, from the outset, doesn't expect to produce a positive cash in flow for you at some stage, and I appreciate that this sounds blindingly obvious, but many people just don't get this.

Just imagine this was a different type of business – let's say a high street coffee shop. Would anybody in their right mind sell the coffee for less than it cost to make it (other than for a very short-term promotional activity)? I don't think so! So why do people think it's OK to do the same with property? Sadly, many people think that it's OK to subsidise the property on a monthly basis as a sacrifice for the capital gain in property values, and that's naïve. If we return to the coffee shop business again it's like saying, "I'm going to lose money on all the coffee I sell, day in and day out, in return for some profit on cake sales at the weekend." Overall, the result is not good enough! With a sound strategy, good selection and the right skills you can make money on the coffee *and* the cake; on the monthly income *and* the capital gain.

Don't sell yourself short!

I have had so many people say to me that property investing doesn't work, and when I question them, it seems that the majority have bought a property where they weren't certain of a tenant (never do that – I'll show you a fail-safe technique to guarantee tenants in the next section), or the rent paid by the tenant didn't cover the outgoings: the mortgage and other costs.

And I say, "So why did you buy it, then?" And they say a combination of, "It seemed like a good idea at the time", or, "It seemed so easy when I watched them doing it on the telly", or, "I thought I'd just top up the shortfall each month out of my salary."

The sad thing is that amateur investors don't realise that the 'top it up out of my salary route' is the sure-fire route to eventual bankruptcy, so while you are in my care you are *never, ever* allowed to buy any rental property that doesn't produce a positive cash flow on a regular basis.

I understand that there may be occasions when it doesn't: a tenant swap-over, change of strategy on your part, timing, typhoon or tornado, but as a general rule *don't* buy anything without making sure that the rent covers all costs on a monthly basis – or I will come and find you at night.

So be afraid!

I will cover the rental calculations, and the approach you will need to safeguard your cash for capital strategies, refurbishment, renovation etc., in the income section.

For now, enough said: just make sure your properties generate *cash flow*.

Yield

Often when you start looking at property as an investment, you get presented with this figure that people call yield. It's a simple figure, and is useful when you first look at a property as it gives you a general sense of what the property does. It's also useful in those initial review stages of comparing one property against another because the property with the highest quoted yield would, on the face of it anyway, be the better deal.

However, that's all the yield is really useful for, and I think we need to take the yield as a general guide before we get more specific with evaluating the individual properties.

The reason I'm not a fan of the yield calculation is because it doesn't really mean much to me and my money in the deal. I know a lot of 'sophisticated' investors like it, and agents also quote it, but it has nothing to do with me, so as I can't influence it, I don't use it as a measure.

So how is it calculated?

It's a simple percentage calculated by taking the gross rent as a proportion of the property value. If the property is worth £200,000 and it generates rent of £1,000 per month, or £12,000 per year, the yield is then:

★ £12,000/£200,000 X100 =6% ★

There are slight variations to this: sometimes yield is calculated on the purchase price of the property, and sometimes the rent is *net* rent (after costs) as opposed to the gross yield calculated above. And that's it.

It's more commonly used in commercial property transactions and I'm really a straightforward residential property girl, so it has never really had an impact on me.

Furthermore, I don't like its lack of accountability to me as an investor. So, if the value of the property goes up 10% due to the property market overall (which even I can't influence), while the rent stays the same, my yield drops to:

£12,000/£200,000 + 10% (£220,000) x 100 = 5.45%

That hardly seems fair to me, so I would much rather use measures and figures that I can impact.

For me, property is about me and my ability to be good at it. I measure that by return on my cash investment and the effort I make, and not the external situation that the yield represents.

Mortgages

I get so many questions about mortgages that I feel I need to start at the top here and explain mortgages in full.

But before we start, it is worth thinking about mortgages from the finance providers' or lenders' perspective. All financial providers at some time have money to lend; in fact there is more money out there waiting to find borrowers than there is demand from us to borrow that money.

Each financial service provider is in business to make money and constantly has business targets to meet; they actually need to be providing mortgages or they go bust. You've only got to look at the amount of advertising, marketing and direct mail shots they all generate to know that statement is true.

So put yourself in their place, as this acts as a massive motivation for them to loan you money – just imagine that! They really, really want to be able to provide you with investment money; all you have to do is ask for it – and ask for it in the right way.

On top of that, there are many thousands of different financial service products out there waiting for you. There are mortgages for the self-employed, for the unemployed and for the fully employed. There are mortgages for old people, young people, groups of people, pairs and individuals. There *will* be a financial product out there that suits your particular situation and circumstances – you may have to search through perhaps seven thousand sources to find it, but it *will* be there!

As a guide, just go into a search engine on the web and type in a particular funding type, say, 'bad credit mortgages', and see what pops up! I am constantly amazed by the variety and number of different funding options there are. I am sure that there will be some provider who specialises in funding for every type of person and every type of strategy.

Remember: there is more money out there waiting to be borrowed than there is demand for that money – so get some today.

So what are the basic mortgage types?

There are two basic groups of mortgages: those that include an element of capital in each repayment (which is normally monthly) and those that don't.

Repayment Mortgage

This is the 'old-fashioned' mortgage that most of us know and love. Many of us have had a repayment mortgage in the past. The repayment mortgage is normally over a twenty-five-year term (but can be any period in length), in which each monthly payment made includes an interest element and a capital element. The interest is charged on the principal (or capital) amount outstanding, and the capital is repaid over the period of the mortgage. Although the monthly payment amounts don't vary significantly over the term, at the beginning of these mortgages the monthly payment is almost entirely interest and by the end of the term, the monthly payment is almost entirely capital.

However, it is worth noting that over the twenty-five years of these mortgages the total repayments typically amount to two or three times the original capital loan amount, so the total repayments over twenty-five years on a £100,000 loan would probably be in excess of £250,000.

Interest-Only Mortgage

An interest-only mortgage does exactly what it says on the tin! It is where your monthly repayment covers only the interest on the principal borrowed over the course of the mortgage term. In some cases there is separate provision made to accumulate an amount equal to the capital principle borrowed, such that when the term of the mortgage ends, there is a lump sum somewhere available to pay off the original loan. Endowments are one form of this, ISA (or PEP) mortgages are another, and pension mortgages are a third. In all of these cases, some extra money per month goes into some other savings vehicle that is expected to generate a sufficient return to produce a sizeable lump sum after time.

However, these additional capital-producing products are not compulsory when taking out an interest-only mortgage.

Which To Use?

Now, I can't give you advice, and the Financial Conduct Authority would ask that you go and see a personal financial advisor to find out the exact solution for you. I agree with that – and I'm certainly not going to comment on what you should do for your domestic, residential mortgage.

But for investment or buy-to-let properties, investors often want to go for interest-only borrowings as it increases their ROCI; after all, they are in this for business reasons and want to generate the highest return they can.

Mortgage Affordability Criteria

In 2014, the UK financial services industry introduced the MMR or Mortgage Market Review, more commonly known as the mortgage affordability criteria, and this means that if you want to take out a mortgage for the purchase of a domestic, residential home then you need to provide all sorts of information showing that you can afford the mortgage repayments, and that may include disclosing what you spend on beer, hairdressing and gym memberships, for instance.

It is worth noting, however, that these criteria do not apply to investment or buy-to-let mortgages.

Overall the mortgage market is becoming more and more regulated, and so knowledge is vital here.

It is absolutely no coincidence that the rapid increase of peer-to-peer lending (which now runs into the billions), private lending, angel financing and other types of creative financing has occurred at the same time as the more traditional and public borrowing methods have become more heavily regulated and difficult to obtain.

And this is a good thing for professional investors over amateurs. Amateurs don't have access to these non-traditional forms of finance in the main because they require information, knowledge and experience to master.

How Many Mortgages Can I Have? Answer Number One

The answer is, as many as you like.

There is no legal limit on the number of mortgages or the number of properties you can own, but it all depends on the criteria of the lenders. Some lenders will only provide you with, say, ten mortgages, some say they will lend you up to a maximum of £5 million in total and others say something else.

Some lenders don't mind if you use other lenders as well – so you could have two or three or more providers and use all of their individual limits.

It also varies with time, and during the credit crunch period between 2008 and 2013 it's fair to say that a lot of lenders closed their doors or severely restricted their lending criteria; but during 2014 the doors started to open again and there are many more products available for investment funding.

In summary, when the economy is flat or negative the lenders restrict what they will lend and when the economy is growing and doing well, the lenders relax their approach and lend you more, with different products and options available.

Recently, we have seen a flood of longer-term fixed-rate mortgage products at ridiculously low rates. You can even get some ten-year fixed-rate products at less than 5%, which is extraordinary, and if you are of a cautious nature, you can invest in property and fix your mortgage rate and funding costs for the next decade.

In all honesty, if you do this property investing properly you could complete your portfolio in ten years and know for certain what your funding costs would be for the entire lifespan of your investing – how amazing is that?

How Many Mortgages Can I Have? Answer Number Two

The second answer here relates to an individual property and how many mortgages you can have on one single property – and again the answer is as many as you like.

There is no legal limit to how many mortgages you can have on one property as long as the individual lenders are informed and agree.

Some lenders only want to be the first on the list (having the first charge over the property), some are OK with having the second or third charge and being lower down the list, but in essence you can keep mortgaging one single property again and again.

That might not make financial sense, and it's generally always easier to go back to the first lender if you need more funds, but many investors do multiple mortgages and remortgages because it's much easier to raise finance on something you already own as opposed to something you don't yet own.

To put that into investing context, what professionals do is this:

- Buy property number one with a standard deposit and a mortgage.
- Do something to the property to increase its value, or even wait until it goes up in value with the market trend.
- Remortgage the property, pay off the first mortgage, get a new mortgage for an increased amount and use the spare money generated to provide the deposit for properties two and three, and so on.

Let's say you buy an investment property for £100,000 with a 75% LTV mortgage and you put in £25,000 of your own money as the deposit.

After a while, and after you do the property up, you find that the property is now worth £150,000.

If you go and get a 75% LTV mortgage now on the property, either with the original lender or with someone else, you will now get a mortgage for: 75/100 x £150,000 = £112,500.

You take the £112,500 and pay off the first mortgage of £75,000, leaving yourself with £37,500 (£112,500 – £75,000) to put into property number two.

Then, if we wind that theory forward, you can see that after a time you now have *two* properties that you can remortgage and release money from, which can provide the deposits to buy properties three and four in your portfolio. And then you do it again and again.

Now, if you take this route to creating a property portfolio you only have to find the deposit for property number one yourself; all the others come from the properties themselves.

What happens here is that the properties in the developing portfolio become self-funding. Many people worry about where they will find the money to buy a dozen or so properties whereas, in fact, the only real challenge is finding the deposit for the *first* one.

The Issue of Repaying the Mortgage

This section is for our debt-hating mothers.

So let's assume that you purchase your properties with interest-only buy-to-let mortgages. How do the mortgages get repaid?

For most professional property investors that depends on their strategies, as follows:

- If they do not intend to hold the property for the full length of the mortgage (say, twenty-five years) they can repay the mortgage principal from any sales proceeds when they sell it.

Example: I buy a property in 2004 for £100,000 with a 75% mortgage. I sell it in 2012 for £200,000.

Purchase:

Mortgage is:	£75,000, so 75/100 x £100,000
My deposit is:	£25,000

Sale:

Proceeds:	£200,000
Less mortgage:	£75,000
Gain in my pocket:	**£125,000**

- However, a professional investor is unlikely to have just one property and so this repayment out of sales proceeds can also happen across the portfolio. The sale of one might pay off the mortgages for two or more properties elsewhere, when the time is right and as long as it is strategically sensible to do so.

- As the property investor matures their portfolio, they may move some of their mortgages on to repayment mortgages later, and again, this is dependent on strategy. For instance, let's say an investor wants to build up a portfolio of twenty properties over ten years.

  Now, when they start it makes sense to purchase the properties on interest-only mortgages: the cash flow is better and more positive (and we like that!), the ROCI is higher (and we like that too!) and an added benefit is that it's easier for your tax return.

When you are first getting started you need every bit of help you can get and you want to drive out your portfolio and get it fully invested as soon as possible. The more cash you have left over each month for reinvestment into the next property, and the higher your **ROCI** is, the quicker that portfolio gets built.

And then… When it has been built, and you can relax, sit back, admire your work and live off the proceeds, *then* you revert the mortgages to repayment mortgages and start addressing them, paying them off over time.

The challenge with having repayment mortgages in the first place is that it takes a great deal longer to build the portfolio and to get financially free, and consequently, it can actually take longer to pay off the mortgages as you have less opportunity, and less spare cash, to repay the mortgages early.

Remember that, on average, each house is sold every seven years and so there is an opportunity to address the mortgage issue then. It is very unlikely that any property investor would hold a mortgage for its full term.

Summary

We've galloped through a few of the important topics: mortgages, money and the calculations and important numbers to get familiar with before moving on to look at specific properties.

Professional investors should have all these figures at their fingertips and, if you struggle with the maths, you need to either get better or find a friend or group that can help you.

Action Plan

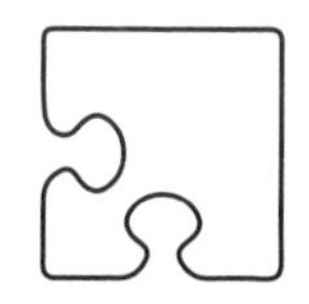

CHAPTER 3

Sourcing For Success

Before we go any further I need to introduce you to two important couples that I know: Dom and Dora and Pete and Pam.

They're fictional couples, and they look identical, but they differ in one important aspect: how they buy property.

Dom and Dora

Let's start with Dom and Dora. They are Dom and Dora Doughnut the Domestic Duo, and they are only interested in buying a property as their residential home.

They are normal: they have two children, one dog called Fido and a lawnmower.

They have a nice three-bedroomed semi-detached house, but they want to trade up and get a bigger house as Dom has been promoted at work and they now have confidence in the economy and Dom's job, so they believe they can afford it.

Where do they start?

They look at property websites. That tells them broadly what to expect from selling their own home, so they add the amount of a larger mortgage to their savings and toddle off to the local estate agent.

1 The local estate agent asks them how much they can afford and the search is on!

2 The agent then asks other vital questions, like number of bedrooms, specific location and whether or not they want a garage or garden.

3 They are then given paper copies of properties that (broadly) fit their criteria and they go viewing.

Now, Dom and Dora nowadays might vary this purchasing strategy a bit by looking in the local paper, or on the Internet at online agencies, but basically the formula is the same: Dom and Dora buy their property based on the following criteria:

- What they can afford?
- Number of bedrooms – can they get a guest room?
- Location and proximity to work and school?

Then:

- Will the kids' bunk beds go in bedroom three?
- Proximity to friends, dance class, Dora's mum?
- Is there somewhere to walk Fido?
- Will the décor go with that lovely sofa they bought in the sales?

And that's all fine and perfectly reasonable as far as purchasing strategies go for them.

Pete and Pam

But let's look at Pete and Pam, who are Pete and Pam Perfect, the Property Partners. They are professional investors and they want to buy a Property for their Portfolio – where do they look?

- On the web, but at different sites. They look at the normal ones for valuation estimates just the same, but then they wander off into sites that sell properties cheaply: auction sites and repossession sites.

- They also phone the local hospitals and universities and speak to the accommodation departments to find out what the students or nurses need, where that accommodation needs to be and even what it looks like.

- They go to property network meetings and talk to other investors to assess the local market, and they may even buy a property there from one of the other investors.

- They speak to the local lettings agents to find out what properties would rent out in the blink of an eye – and where they are – then they go and buy those.

- They look on the local council website to see if they hold a regular landlords' forum and go there, again to find out what's going on locally and to meet other Petes and Pams who may be wishing to sell.

- They may also look on the HMO register to discover which local properties have been turned into HMOs and where they might be.

- They talk to sourcing agents, who will find properties for a fee.

- They might place an advert in the local paper offering to buy properties that fit their investment strategy.

- They go for a walkabout in the area where they think they want to buy, knock on doors and put leaflets through letterboxes asking the current owner to contact them if they want to sell.

- They look in odd places: the church commission, for instance, which may be selling properties or land.

I could go on here, but I'm hoping you get the gist of what Pete and Pam do. They approach the purchasing decision from a **strategic standpoint** and look for properties that fit their **portfolio** and **strategy**.

This is crucial. Pete and Pam highlight an area of potential demand – say, a university – and do their research to see how solid the demand might be. They ask what type of property is needed, where it needs to be and even when it's needed.

Normally, if you look on any university website there will be an accommodation area. You will quickly see where all the students live – or want to live – and the nearer the campus, the better.

Also, think about the lettings agents. Pete and Pam talk to the lettings agents *before* they talk to an estate agent, and they use the lettings agents' experience and local knowledge to tell them which properties could be rented swiftly, identifying demand.

Experienced Investor's Tip

I sometimes get people telling me that property investing doesn't work, and when I ask why they say, "Well, I bought this flat and I can't get a tenant", and my question to them is always the same: "Why did you buy it, then?"

The big difference between an amateur investor and a professional one is that an amateur will buy a property in the hope of getting a tenant and a professional investor finds the tenant (or the customer for their business) first and then finds a property that fits!

Summary

It is vitally important that we get this issue. Dom and Dora and Pete and Pam are the same people to look at, but their objectives are different and the way they find property is different.

Dom and Dora focus on the *supply* of available properties and Pete and Pam focus on where there is *demand* for their investment strategy and for their product.

Dom and Dora are guided by what they can afford and Pete and Pam aren't – they are guided by strategy, rates of return, profitability, cash flow and business criteria, and that's the real crux of this session.

It bothers me that people think they know about property investing because they all live somewhere! Most people have some experience in that they have either rented or purchased their own home, and they think that gives them an insight into what property investing is about – it doesn't!

I wish in some way that a property you bought for investment looked different than those you buy to live in, but it doesn't – it looks just like the same – but they are as different as chalk and cheese.

One is bought with emotion and one is bought without emotions. Theoretically, you don't even need to physically see an investment property in order to work out if it fits your portfolio or business, and I do have properties that I have never seen or visited – but beware! *Somebody* looked at those properties for me, so make sure all properties are viewed, even if it's not by you.

Dom and Dora buy property as a home where they sleep at night and Pete and Pam buy cash-generating business units – it's fundamental that you understand the difference.

Where to Invest

Before we get into the different types of investment strategy, we need to consider where we should start looking to find the ideal investment property, and one of the most frequent questions I get from people when they start investing is about where they should buy property. In all honesty, I struggle to answer as it's a fundamentally flawed question.

There is no ideal place to buy just as there isn't any ideal time to start – you may as well just get on with it, and *now*.

The concept that there is a geographical place and a specific address like 27 Acacia Avenue that is the perfect investment is clearly both a ridiculous assumption and quite scary, as it illustrates hugely worrying thought patterns for a potential investor.

I have heard many silly stories over the years, including comments like, "Oh, buy-to-let doesn't work in London".

Now think about that – and think about London. It's a big place, and within London there are many different areas: there's Hampstead and St John's Wood and the posh places, then there's the East End and South London that aren't so posh – and then within the East End there's the area around Stratford that has been regenerated as part of the London Olympics and so on. So all over a place as big as London there are widely different properties and property prices, and very specific and localised demand and supply.

Therefore it's daft to say that any investing does or doesn't work in any geographical area overall – as long as you can find one property that works for you somewhere, then it works!

But what we can say is that investing *does* work in some places. For instance, every time I send a letter off to the vehicle licensing centre, the DVLA in Swansea, I think about where all the workers at the DVLA live. There must be thousands of them, mustn't there? And they all need to live somewhere – so my guess is that the part of Swansea near the DVLA must be a good investing environment.

Furthermore, if you can find a good property in the road next to a university campus, that *will* work, and likewise, how about a nice house next to a teaching hospital where there might be young medical students and nurses who need to rent somewhere? That'll work too.

Even think about a flat next to a retail or leisure park. There must be lots of young single people working in the shops and burger bars there who all need to live somewhere cheap – so that will also work.

As you can see, it's not so much a physical geographical location that works but more a *situation* that works.

With this in mind, I have developed a sixteen-point checklist to identify those situations – and consequently those investment opportunities – that will work anywhere.

I have divided the sixteen points into two blocks of eight – one list is general and the second list is specific, so let's start with the general list. I have turned the list into a mnemonic list, so every letter of the word LOCATION represents something we need to look for.

NB: although, in the main, these criteria look to be for income-type strategies only, they can apply to both income and capital strategies, and you'll see later that we always evaluate each potential property against both income and capital criteria just to be safe; to provide us with a contingency and a second exit strategy.

LOCATION

L is for local situation – and here I am looking for the DVLA, or the university, or the teaching hospital, or the retail park, or a school – so I am looking for the one or two streets anywhere where there will be regular, consistent and appropriate demand for the property I want to buy as a potential rental property. It's important to look for these pockets of demand to find the situation that will work for you.

O is for on the road – and what I mean by that is that every property you buy as an investment needs to be fairly near a main road so that the tenant can get in and out easily and access is simple. And with this one you can see that I am aiming at getting at customer volume – or customer demand – and providing a property that would suit most people most of the time. Pretty, little isolated cottages are all very well, but in order to be more certain of my profits and cash flows I need to make sure I can attract a large number of potential customers – and that means ensuring easy access.

C stands for cash flow – we have already covered this, and any business owner will understand this one immediately because without cash flow we are broke, so it's pretty important to make sure that the property will provide you with cash – and sooner rather than later. So, as an ideal, look for properties that are already tenanted as they will provide you with cash flow from day one (but of course, make sure that the rent covers all the monthly expenses before you sign the deal).

A is for analyse the returns, and again, it is vital you do this before you buy as you need to make sure that the investment will provide you with an appropriate regular return, either as monthly rental income or as a capital return if you decide to sell it on quickly. An ideal return is up to you to choose, but I always start with double what I could get in a bank – and at the moment that's pretty low as the average deposit rate in the UK is currently about 1% per year or less, so look for any return that gives you at least higher than twice that on your money.

T stands for tenants – and plenty of them – as these are your customers and the lifeblood of your property. Only ever buy where there's a good regular supply of tenants.

The **I** and the **O** together stand for **I O**, **I O**, it's off to work we go! Because every property you buy has to be close to as many sources of employment as possible: factories, shops, offices, the docks, the DVLA – whatever – and your property also needs to have easy access to those local places of work. You want your tenants to be employed, if possible, and you can help there by having the property close to as many places of employment as possible.

Finally the **N** stands for newspapers, bread and milk, and that means making sure your property is near to some general stores and services – that includes groceries, petrol, a pub, a post office and anything else you think is important. Think about how near you would like those things and set a target; so, for instance, ensure that any property you buy is no more than five minutes' walk from a newspaper, or five minutes' walk from a shop that sells milk and bread.

So, that gives us some general tips on location and, once we have ticked all those boxes, we can go on to the specific checklist of what to look for, and we need to take each letter of the word **SPECIFIC** to find those:

SPECIFIC

S stands for safe – you have to be sure that you would be happy for your mum, dad, brother or sister to be there, particularly at night. And that's because tenants won't go where they don't feel safe, so any property that makes them feel vulnerable won't do.

P stands for plumbing, which has to work! Tenants like power showers, hot water and heating, so you need to check that the plumbing is good or be prepared to pay to fix it.

E stands for external perspective, and any property, even flats, needs some outdoor space if at all possible – so a balcony, share of a garden, a yard or roof terrace. That's because human beings need to see out and get some sense of visual perspective in order to be happy. If you don't have that your tenant will get fed up, miserable and leave – so make sure there is some outdoor space and, preferably, some good external views as well.

C stands for ceilings, which, ideally, should be nice and high and clear, as that will all give a sense of space and brightness.

I stands for internal dimensions and appearance, and I set myself certain targets. For instance, the main bedroom (or the only bedroom) has to be at least one hundred square feet in size – so that's ten foot by ten foot or similar – and any separate living room or reception room needs to be the same, otherwise you can't really get furniture in the rooms. It's OK if second bedrooms or kitchens are not quite that big, but for the main rooms you do need to be able to have furniture and walk about a bit!

F stands for both fitted furniture and fixtures and fittings. This is about getting the best use out of the space available, because if we have relatively small rooms we can create a better space by having as much of the furniture as possible fitted to the wall, leaving a larger floor area visible in the middle – so look for fitted wardrobes, fitted kitchens, fitted bathroom cabinets and so on and regard them as a plus on your checklist.

I stands for intuitive flow. Now, I don't understand feng shui or what it means, but a property, for me, has to be intuitive in that bedrooms generally have to be upstairs and the property needs to flow from the front door to the back door, going through the living space and the kitchen. So we don't want toilets off the lounge, and I don't like properties where the main bedroom is downstairs and the other bedrooms are upstairs – that's daft, as any young parent with a baby or young children will tell you. So a property needs to have logic to it.

C stands for cleanable. It doesn't matter if the property isn't clean when you buy it, but it does need to be capable of being cleaned by a normal human. So if the property smells weird or has masses of condensation, then think carefully because you can't clean away damp. Look and smell for mould, rot and damp – it's generally obvious. Mushrooms are a giveaway – black dots which are often in the corners – or wallpaper that is slipping off a damp wall. None of that can be cleaned with a mop and bucket.

You can still buy these properties but, in that case, you are looking at a longer-term capital project where the tenant can't move in quickly, and those types of properties will be covered in the next chapter.

There we have it; sixteen things to look for: eight general **LOCATION** factors, and eight **SPECIFIC** ones. You will probably realise that all of the items on the checklists are about having a property that most people will find acceptable most of the time – for me it's all about maximising the chances of getting a tenant and getting the best financial return for the property. We can only do that if we have volume and lots of options, so the more you can buy properties that will appeal to the masses, the better.

Then, of course, we need to avoid the situations – or places – that don't work, and again I have a mnemonic that will direct you, and this time it's the words **NO SALES**.

NO SALES

Let's start with the **N** then, which stands for noise and nuisance. We can include in that any challenging or inconvenient situation.

Obviously, in the noise category, we can include airports, major roads, taxi ranks, railway stations, bus terminals and so on. We know that we want our properties to be close to some communication links but we don't want them right at the end of runway two at Heathrow – so we need to watch that.

The issue with noise is that it doesn't seem important until you have it – and then it becomes a relentless sleep-stopper

– and in those circumstances your tenants won't stay very long and you'll be constantly having to replace tenants, which is when lettings become expensive.

Include social challenges such as nightclubs, late-night bars and, possibly, popular restaurants.

Then add to that people noise. See if you can find out a little about the neighbours – do you have a warring couple next door? One of my tenants was next door to a couple who were constantly trying to bash each other and the police were often called. My tenant said it was like listening to *EastEnders* on a constant basis, and at first he was amused and used to listen at the wall with a glass to his ear, but it soon got tiresome.

Then finally, under noise and nuisance, we have the other end of the scale: children, bless 'em. Children are weird – your own are lovely but other people's are a bit more irritating. So even if you do have kids, or want kids, please don't buy the house right next door to the school, otherwise you'll have no glass in the back windows, you won't be able to park at 3.15 and you'll be forever kicking the ball back.

Even devoted and child-friendly folks don't want to live right next door to the school or park; up the road maybe, or the next street, but not right next door.

So I hope that gives you some idea of the noise and nuisance you may encounter – and need to avoid. In many cases the nuisance or noise is obvious, like an airport for instance, but in other cases it's not so transparent and so I always suggest walking down at different times of the day. Also speak to neighbours, if you can, before you buy. It could be that the property is on a shortcut through from a local nightclub or something and so every Friday and Saturday night, at four in the morning, there are always people singing outside.

O in our **NO SALES** mnemonic stands for *odd one out* – or the *oddity property.*

What I mean by that is purely the oddball property in the street, the property that's out of line with the others locally or the property that's just in the wrong place. You can easily spot these, as they'll be the residential property in a retail area or in an industrial or commercial area.

I recently saw advertised a beautiful country mansion property worth about £1.5m and it was selling for only £395k – because it was slap bang in the middle of an industrial estate.

Another version of this odd one out is when you get a property that's different to all the others in the street – particularly if it's the best property in the street. The challenge with those is that the capital increase, or uplift, is more difficult to achieve – you're much better off going with the worst house in the street; at least then you know how far you can uplift its value, which is to the value of the best house in the street.

The overall problem with oddball properties is that although you will certainly be able to buy them cheaper, you'll always have a limited number of potential tenants and potential buyers, and anything that makes your life more difficult as an investor should be avoided if you can.

S stands for *structural problems*, and I include in that any underpinning or subsidence issues, major external cracking or other significant damage. These are for the construction specialists and other experts and not for the faint-hearted – or me!

I wouldn't do it for two main reasons: firstly, I don't have the expertise, and secondly, these projects take up a lot of time and money and I like to keep my time and money moving quickly.

However, I must say that if you're a structural engineer or someone with that kind of expertise then this *can* be a good strategy – but for the rest of us there are easier projects to manage.

A stands for *above the chip shop*. This is just another version of the oddities really, as a flat above a chip shop, or any retail food outlet, is a residential in a retail area and hence an oddball in my books – but food outlets are particularly challenging for three reasons:

Firstly, the *aroma* – chip shops smell lovely on a Friday night after a night out, but smell less attractive and more greasy on a sunny Saturday morning. Secondly, these outlets have a lot of food rubbish, which in turn attracts a lot of rats and vermin.

So, aroma, rubbish and rats – avoid them!

L stands for *listed* – and this is because, like properties with structural problems, they require specialist knowledge that I don't have.

A listed building is one that has been placed on the Statutory List of Buildings of Special Architectural or Historic Interest. It is widely used and applies to around half a million buildings.

A listed building may not be touched (demolished, extended or altered) without permission from the local planning authority, which usually consults the relevant central government agency, particularly for significant alterations to the more notable listed buildings.

There are three types of listed buildings in England and Wales:

- Grade I: buildings of exceptional interest.
- Grade II*: buildings that are of special interest, warranting every effort to preserve them.
- Grade II: particularly important buildings of more than special interest.

And they are, in all likelihood, wonderful properties, but the challenge is in the permissions needed to alter, enhance and improve, which means that dealing with these properties is incredibly time-consuming and restrictive.

Look at them by all means, but don't invest in them unless you have specialist knowledge – and lots of spare money!

E stands for *environmental*, and boy, is there a lot here.

Now, I don't know much about science or about environmental issues in detail, and I don't know whether electricity masts cause childhood leukaemia or not – but what I do know is that most people worry, to a greater or lesser degree, about the effects of pollution, flooding, radon, masts and so on. Therefore, any property with any of these issues is best avoided because the presence of any environmental issue or concern automatically reduces my market of potential tenants and buyers – and my selling price.

Things to look out for are: aerials, pylons, masts, electricity sub-stations and all things electronic.

Then there's flooding: flood plains, flood defences and rising sea levels. To check for those, the environment agency (www.environment-agency.gov.uk) has a series of interactive maps so you can see where areas at risk of flooding and pollution, etc. are.

And the list goes on – for example, you may want to check for radon, or landfill sites. If you just put the issue at hand into a search engine you will get someone or other who will tell you where the problems are. So for radon, for example, look at www.ukradon.org and you'll get a location map.

There are also specific issues in different parts of the country; for instance, watch out for mining and shafts in parts of Cornwall.

Once you have checked all of the different types of environmental challenge you can think of, one good extra test is to go on to the web and try to get an insurance quote. If there are any environmental issues near to the property you are looking at, the insurance premium will be higher, and often insurance companies are a lot quicker and more attuned than most to picking up these issues.

Now finally, we are down to the last **S** in **NO SALES**, and this one summarises some of the other categories, and that's please don't buy anything *scary*!

In the scary category we can obviously include anything environmental, since some people find pylons scary. Also, we can include some of the noise and nuisance issues here – again, drunken crowds from a local nightclub can be scary.

But in addition to all the things we have already covered, just have one final look around the area before you buy a property – does it look OK? Is it light and open as an area, or are there dark alleys?

Does it look easy to get to the property from the bus stop or train station – even late at night?

One good measure is always to ask yourself, "Would I be happy for a member of my family to live there?" Would you feel safe with that? If so, that will tell you it's OK to buy for a potential tenant.

I hope that you can hear that none of these issues are personal prejudices but are all circumstances or situations that would reduce the demand in my property investing business. What we need in order to be successful in this arena is a steady and consistent volume of customers who want to rent, because the properties are our business product that we are trading.

Ideally, to make our business as viable, profitable and secure as possible, we want volume – and that will only be achieved if you get properties that most people are happy with most of the time. That means avoiding anything that puts people off – or results in **NO SALES**!

Summary of Location Criteria

We have now got a list of things we would embrace and a list of things to avoid when buying a property for investment. Although we are going to concentrate first on income properties most of these 'yes' and 'no' criteria are equally relevant for the investor who wants to buy and sell for capital gain.

And that's important as a contingency because even if our intention is to rent the property out, if something goes wrong with that plan, it is important to have a separate backup plan ready – or a second exit strategy for the property – which, in most cases, would be to resell.

Checklists: download them for use as a summary for your property purchasing. Copies are available from: www.fieldingfinancial.com/propertypuzzle.

When purchasing look for:

LOCATION SPECIFIC

- ☐ **Local situation** that indicates demand.
- ☐ **On the road** – it needs to have transport and communication links.
- ☐ **Cash flow** – does it give you any?
- ☐ **Analyse** the returns on the all-important numbers.
- ☐ **Tenants** – and lots of them!
- ☐ **I O, I O, it's off to work we go** – employment sources.
- ☐ **Newspapers** – near to facilities and supplies.
- ☐ **Safe** to live in.
- ☐ **Plumbing**.
- ☐ **External space** – is there somewhere to get outside?
- ☐ **Ceilings** high/sense of space.
- ☐ **Internal dimensions** that are big enough, and rooms fit for purpose.
- ☐ **Furniture, fixtures and fittings** – do they contribute to the best use of the property?
- ☐ **Intuitive flow** and logic to a house layout.
- ☐ **Cleanable** and presentable: if it isn't now, could you make it so?

When purchasing, avoid:

NO SALES

- ☐ **Noise and nuisance**.
- ☐ **Oddity properties** – out of keeping with their environment.
- ☐ **Structural damage** in properties.
- ☐ **Aroma! (above the chip shop)** – remember, aroma, rubbish and rats!
- ☐ **Listed buildings**.
- ☐ **Environmental issues**.
- ☐ **Scary places**.

CHAPTER 4

Investing For Income

For most people the objective in property investing is to become financially free – or at least be in a position to have financial choices.

For many that means being able to give up the day job, but for others who might love that day job, it's a case of having enough money for good holidays, a new car, to give to the children – or maybe they just want to give it all away to the local church, charity or cats' home.

All of those objectives are fine as long as they're a conscious choice and create a strategy that works for you. What doesn't work is having no choice or options and being stuck in a rat race, with a job that you can't get out of, and having no financial freedom either now or in the future.

It follows then that for most people the income strategy should be the first one to embark on. I often say that you don't go broke banking cheques every month and – as long as you do this strategy properly – that's exactly what you get.

I have already made my point about negative cash flow, so we're looking for a property that provides enough rent to pay all the expenses, give us some spare, or contingency, and then put some money in our pockets every month as well.

And then you do that as many times as you need to provide enough monthly income to pay all your living expenses; your personal gas bill, and feed the children – and that's financial freedom.

Basic Buy-to-Let

The basic income-producing strategy is the buy-to-let. This area of the market has attracted enormous attention in recent years in the UK. There have been many financial products, books and TV programmes centred around buy-to-let, and there is even a regular magazine called *Landlord & Buy-to-Let Magazine* – but what does it mean?

Clearly, in simple terms, the process is about buying a property that you rent out to someone – a tenant. The attraction is that the tenant pays rent, which ideally covers your mortgage and other costs such that, at the end of the day, the property becomes yours. The property has been purchased for you and paid for by someone else.

The starting point is to determine which type of buy-to-let property you want to buy: is it a one-bedroom flat for professional tenants, family accommodation or even a HMO for students? It is essential that you decide this before you even start looking for that property, because you need to purchase a completely different dwelling for different eventual tenants.

What type of tenant would we like?

- **Singles**: even within this category we have a variety of options. Do we want to attract manual or blue collar workers, or semi-professional office workers or upmarket professionals? In each case the property looks different and is in a different location. So, for the blue collar workers, the property needs to be very close to potential employment sources. The potential tenant may work unusual hours or shifts, so they need to be within walking distance of their job. The tenant may not have huge amounts of money so the property needs to be clean but perhaps basic, and the rent will be at the lower range.

  The property for a semi-professional tenant is slightly different and slightly more upmarket. It can be close to transport links that go to the business or financial centre of the local town. It is likely that this property will produce an average rental income.

  The property for a professional tenant will be the most expensive but will generate the highest rent. This property will be well maintained and of a high standard of décor. It is likely that it will have a garage, or parking space, and perhaps a security entrance system.

Although these three definitions are 'broad brush' and simplistic, it does provide some general guidelines to bear in mind.

- **Couples or twos**: mainly we can group couples and two people sharing into the same general categories as singles. However, the difference is that – certainly for the sharers – the property needs to have two bedrooms, so it needs to be bigger!

  It is likely that tenants in this category are more likely to be saving up to buy their own home, and perhaps the sharers will be hoping to get their own property, so it is possible that the length of tenancies will be shorter than for singles.

- **Families**: for families, you need to provide safe and comfortable accommodation with children in mind. It is likely that the property will have at least three bedrooms. It's possible that the family is in transition between homes, or perhaps relocating due to employment.

  The property needs to be easily maintained and have a garden and garage. It will be close to the local schools, and the park, the swimming pool and the local swings! The house will be in a fairly private area of town, where there is not a lot of traffic, as the children need to be kept safe at all times.

- **Corporate lets**: a corporate let occurs when companies rent properties for their (usually senior) executives. Tenancies may be for long periods and are generally paid, or guaranteed, by the company. So they are good tenancies and the rents are high, but the property needs to be of the highest quality and in the prime location.

- **Multiple sharers**: these properties will obviously be larger and divided up in some way, for either many unconnected persons, or possibly for a large group of connected people such as students or people who work together, such as nurses. In this case the property needs to be robust, as it will suffer heavy usage. It will need to be located close to where your potential tenant needs to be – so close to the university campus or hospital. In both of these cases (students and nurses) they need to get back and forth frequently and on foot, and perhaps at unusual times of the day or night.

HMOs

An HMO is a House in Multiple Occupation, and is a property that is divided up into several units. It can be a property with four bedrooms that is, for example, shared by four nurses, or it can be a sixteen-bedroomed property that is divided into sixteen bedsits for students. HMOs include properties for asylum seekers and even rooming houses.

So an HMO is any property which has several tenants and which is occupied by a non-standard family unit. The number that constitutes 'multiple' is a subject of some debate and you need to check the definition very carefully with your local HMO office, which you will find at the local housing office. To find this, look in the *Yellow Pages* or ask at the local library or Citizens Advice Bureau.

It is important to know how the definition is determined as, with HMOs, there are separate regulations regarding fire safety and security. You need to comply with these, so get a copy of the regulations and make sure that you understand what you are getting into here.

For most HMOs you, as an individual, will need to be licenced to rent out a specific property – and you need one licence for each property and in each separate area.

HMO Licencing was introduced in the Housing Act 2004, which defined an HMO as a property which:

- Is occupied by more than one household, and where more than one household shares, or lacks, an amenity, such as a bathroom, toilet or cooking facilities.
- Is occupied by more than one household and which is a converted building, but not entirely into self-contained flats (whether or not some amenities are shared or lacking).
- Is converted self-contained flats, but does not meet, as a minimum standard, the requirements of the 1991 Building Regulations, and at least one-third of the flats are occupied under short tenancies.

That licence comes with a fee and it's generally about £200 per year per property, so remember to factor that into your financial evaluation.

Finally, you need to investigate what's known as Article Four, which is a change in legislation, brought in by the government in April 2010, enabling a local council to restrict or limit the number of HMOs in their patch. This followed the creation of a new classification of shared property, C4, which could be treated differently under planning rules.

Councils have used this to control the number of HMOs in their area, to designate certain areas to be HMOs and prohibit other areas completely from establishing HMO properties.

Article Four has impacted some areas more than others.

Please contact the local council about Article Four, the HMO regulations and licencing *and* the possibility of needing planning permission in the area before you even start looking – you could find that HMOs just don't work in a certain place.

However, if you have the time, energy and inclination to battle the red tape here, the returns can be very high. Instead of receiving one rent of, say, £650 per month for your four-bedroom house, you may be able to get, say, four times £250 (a total of £1,000) per month from four nurses.

So HMOs can be a massive income generator but, as always, do your research fully before you embark on this strategy and, to get you started, my three main tips are:

- Location is key – neither students, nor nurses, nor any person who needs to live in an HMO can be very far from where they need to go, as they are unlikely to have their own transport. Therefore, these properties need to be only a few streets away from the college campus or the hospital and suitable amenities.

- Get very specific with your strategy and buy the right property for the proposed tenant. A house for four sharing nurses is quite different to a house full of unconnected students. You need to consider how they live and what that means in terms of property layout, room size, communal areas, bathrooms and kitchens. If you don't know how students or nurses live just ask a letting agent to show you around a few potential properties and you will soon learn.

- The legalities need to be watertight and you need to take extra care with the tenancy agreement, any house-sharing agreement and the taking up of references. You are also more likely to be asking for parental guarantees in the case of young people and students, so make sure that you get everything in place.

The HMO tends to be the mainstay of the professional investor's portfolio.

Evaluation for Income

When setting your income strategy, the easiest way to start is with a target amount you need to generate per month, or per year, and then work out how to get it.

Always remember that there are many ways to achieve income, dependent on your investment strategy, your approach to risk, your financial and personal position and your personality! If you wish to achieve £1,000 per month income you have the choice to generate this from ten little flats producing £100 per month each or perhaps from one HMO generating the full amount, or a variety of options in between. Only you can fully determine the appropriate position for you.

But before you start, learn how to evaluate income properties so that you can measure your profit and performance. It is vital that you do this otherwise you will not know if you are on track with your goals, or your finances.

Please note: when you are thinking about buying a property for income generation you do all the income assessments – as shown below – *first*. We cover the other one-off costs later, like legal fees and stamp duty, but there's no point even thinking about that if the property you are looking at doesn't 'work' financially on a month by month basis.

Financial Assessment of Income Strategies

Wash Its Face, Version One

As we have already discovered, any rental property must cover itself, with the rental income being more than the sum of all the associated costs. If that works then I say that the property 'washes its face'.

In this evaluation, you just take all the inflows and deduct all the outflows and see what is left.

	Per month £
Rental income	....
Less:	
Funding costs	....
Insurances	....
Management fees	....
Gas and safety checks	....
Other costs	....
Net cash inflow/outflow	________

Once you get to the net cash inflow/outflow stage above, you then set your target. Do you just want this to be zero, or at best plus £1? Or do you want this to be £100 per month, £200 or more?

But it has to be cash positive!

For simplicity, when I'm first looking at a potential deal I just take:

The rent
Less: mortgage costs
Less: 10% of rent as a management fee allowance
Less: another 10% of rent to cover everything else

And when I'm really working broad-brush (often when I'm in a cafe opposite a property I've just looked at and writing on a serviette), all I do is take the estimated rent, less mortgage costs, less a guess at 20% of rent.

If any of those simple versions work, and give me what I want, then I continue on to version two of 'Wash its Face', which is more detailed.

Wash Its Face, Version Two

For all income evaluations, once you have done the standard review, and the property appears to work financially, then make your calculations personal and make sure that you include the costs that are relevant to you and your investment strategy.

So, for example, if you need to delegate all the management to an agency, allocate a percentage of the rent as a management fee. However, if you are going to manage all your investment properties yourself, you need to make a different allowance for specific costs incurred.

Also, add in the costs of things such as insurances and maintenance contracts to suit you and your approach to risk and time. You can get insurances that cover

- Buildings.
- Contents.
- Damage by tenants.
- Void periods in your tenancies.
- You can also get regular maintenance contracts for:
  - General maintenance.
  - Plumbing and heating.
  - Cleaning and repair.
  - Gas safety (you *must* have this covered somehow).

But think about it. The more cost you add in to your personal standard evaluation of a property, the less individual properties will be profitable so, at some stage, you need to take a deep breath and consider how much risk you're prepared to take. If you have a need to cover *all* costs and *all* maintenance contracts and *every* type of insurance then you will have to look a lot harder to find a deal that will work where the rent covers all those costs.

Also, size is important here.

If you only have one, two, three or even five properties you could be at more risk. If you have three and one property is empty, that's a problem – if you have nineteen and one is empty that's less of a problem because the remaining eighteen properties pay for the 'problem' property at the time.

Crucial Understanding

At this stage, what you do is make the property and its cash flow specific to *you*. You might be more cautious and want a contingency in there for voids or repairs. You might be a better negotiator and get your management fee down to 7% – or a worse one and pay 20%. You might want all kinds of insurances in there for tenant damage or you may be content just to insure the building.

The key point is this – *you* create the portfolio according to you and your mindset, attitude to risk, personal circumstances (for instance, are you the only breadwinner with a family of six children, or are you single?) and your personality.

If you get that then you will see that one property will work and generate cash flow for some people but not for others, because each person will be putting in different numbers in this Wash its Face calculation and creating different answers, with some people generating a positive cash flow and others a negative one.

So if anyone ever says to you, "That property doesn't work", what they mean is that it doesn't work for *them* – but it still might just work for you.

So get very personal and very specific here. Concentrate on what you want and need and not on what others say; after all, people are constantly telling me that property investing doesn't work – yeah, right!

Return on our Cash Invested

We have already briefly considered this in the money section, but to apply it to our income property we do the following:

Start with the Wash its Face version two calculation above – and if we put some illustrative figures in that, for a property that we buy on a 75% LTV mortgage costing £150,000, it would look like this:

	Per month
	£
Rental income	1,000.00
Less:	
Funding costs (5% interest-only mortgage)	468.75
Insurances (estimate)	35.00
Management fees	100.00
Gas and safety checks	10.00
Other costs	6.25
Net cash inflow/outflow	**380.00**

Now if we take that monthly excess of £380 and multiply it by twelve we will get the annual profit for this property of £4,560.

To calculate our magic **ROCI** figure all we now need to do is to express this annual rent as a percentage of our money in the deal, which in this case is 25% (the deposit) of the purchase price of £150,000: £37,500. The calculation is as follows: £4,560/£37,500 x 100 = 12.16%.

And there is our vital **ROCI**!

We can now evaluate this potential property against other similar properties and pick the one with the highest **ROCI**, and we will continue to return to this measure throughout the time that we hold this particular property.

Experienced Investor's Tip

If you are an experienced investor and used to calculating funding costs you will realise that actually the ROCI in this instance is also our maximum cost of capital. So the ROCI of 12.16% is the maximum we could pay to borrow this deposit money and the deal still work.

ROCI and Remortgage

Let's pull a few things together.

We know that return on our cash is the vital measure, because if a property doesn't give us a decent return on our money what's the point?

We also know now (with a few caveats of course) that mortgages are OK and, curiously, the more we borrow the higher the percentage return on our money – so the bigger the mortgage, the higher our ROCI.

> It sounds a bit counter-intuitive, so let's go through another illustration involving a remortgage, and I'm going to use our earlier example for a property that we bought for £150,000 with a 75% LTV mortgage, meaning that our deposit was £37,500.
>
> We know that our cash flow on that was £380 and our ROCI was 12.16%.
>
> Now let's move the example on to Stage Two: remortgage.
>
> In this case, a bit of time has passed, we have done the property up a bit and it is now worth £170,000.
>
> What happens to our figures if we remortgage at that value with a new 75% LTV mortgage, the new mortgage amount now being £127,500 (£170,000 x 75/100 = £127,500)?
>
> Firstly, we have to pay off the first mortgage of £112,500, leaving us with £15,000 (£127,500 – £112,500), which we can put back into our pocket.
>
> At this stage, our outflow on this property is:

The original deposit	£37,500
Less:	
Funds released back on remortgage	£15,000
Funds now in the deal:	£22,500

However, our cash flow has also changed as we have to account for the higher mortgage costs.

If we assume all other costs remain the same, our Wash its Face calculation now looks like this:

	Per month
	£
Rental income	1,000.00
Less:	
Funding costs (5% interest-only mortgage)	531.25
Insurances (estimate)	35.00
Management fees	100.00
Gas and safety checks	10.00
Other costs	6.25
Net cash inflow/outflow	**317.50**

And now if we run our **ROCI** calculation on that, we find that our new return is: £317.50 x 12/£22,500 (the amount we now have in the deal) x 100 = 16.9%

What has happened here?

- We have reduced our personal financial exposure to £22,500.

- We have reduced our cash flow, but it's still positive (we wouldn't do this if it made the cash flow negative!).

- We have increased the return on our cash invested from 12.16% to 16.9%.

But we have increased our borrowings – and if that bothers you (or your mum), please go back and reread the bit about paying off mortgages.

Overall the impact of this remortgage is advantageous for our property investing business.

Advanced Investor's Thought

If you kept doing this, eventually you would have no money in the deal at all – and then your return is infinite.

That is one reason why experienced and advanced property investors always get a much higher return on their money than novices, because they've had longer to run the remortgage part of their strategy. Consequently, you get better at property investing the higher your target return needs to be – but I'm jumping ahead to the strategy section!

Getting Perfect Tenants

Now, I love tenants – they are my customers, they are my cash producers, they create the turnover for my property business and frankly, they feed me and my kids.

So I need to love them.

On the other hand, if it wasn't for the tenants, renting out properties would be a doddle. They can create problems, they can be annoying, and of course, they cost the business money.

A tenant is both your business lifeblood and the leech that sucks it dry at the same time, so it's a balancing act between one end of the spectrum and the other. Whether we love them or hate them, we certainly can't have a property business without them.

So like all things of this nature – where personal issues interact with business ones – it makes sense to have a neutral method, or formula if you like, to deal with the processing of a tenant; and the more professional and independent and unemotional you can make the whole process, the easier it will be for both you and them.

Also, it's worth bearing in mind that the easier you can make the whole process of dealing with tenants, the more profit you will make and, of course, if you can manage the process properly then the tenants tend to stay longer. The longer the tenants stay, the more profit you make and the more efficient that particular tenancy is.

The biggest cost you will have with tenanting property is the changeover of tenancies, and if you are having to get new tenants in every six months then you're doing something wrong – and certainly you are incurring too much cost.

So having said all that, what are **my top ten tips** for getting and keeping that perfect tenant?

Tip Number One has to be to get a property that tenants want!

Now this actually requires a reasonable level of thought, because not only do we have all the standard criteria of location and communications and access to shops and employment and so on, we also have to bear in mind that each type of tenancy desires a slightly different location and a slightly different type of shop.

So this tip is about getting exactly the right property for the right tenant, and it helps to get really specific here. If you want to rent out one-bedroom flats to professionals you definitely need access to fast communications to the local employment source – but that's not so important for a family let, for instance, where perhaps access to the road to the school and the park is more important.

Experienced Investor's Tip

Advertise!

Many professional investors use the tenant and their knowledge to direct their purchasing strategy; after all, the tenant should be able to tell you exactly what they want. An easy way to get access to the tenant and their requirements is by advertising! So before you even buy anything, take out an ad in the local paper of your location of choice advertising for a tenant. It could say: *Tenant wanted for lovely one-bed property in city centre/down by the church/by the station. (Use whatever specific location you have in mind.) Rent: £750 per month. Phone 0123 456 789.*

There is no lie here – you are not actually advertising a property, you are advertising for a tenant. And when the tenant calls you can explain that and ask what *they* are looking for – and then you buy that!

Now, there are several things to take from this exercise:

- If no one replies to your ad – *don't* buy there.
- If fifty people reply to the ad – go and buy fifty properties to fulfil the demand. Well, OK, maybe not fifty, but ten?
- Speak to the respondent and ask exactly what they want. Also, ask if they have seen a property they like. Ask if they know if it's up for sale. There's always the chance that they know exactly and all you need to do is to send the tenant round to view and then phone up the agent and buy it!

If you're really lucky with this exercise you may even get a potential tenant to go and find the property for you; then you certainly will have a good tenant because if they've chosen the exact property they want, then it's likely they will stay a long time – and frankly there's no difference for us as investors between one particular property or another as long as it fits the pyramid, washes its face and so on.

Also use this exercise to test your rent levels, using two or more ads that have the same text but at different rent levels, say, £750, £850 and so on. See how many responses you get at each level to help you fix your price.

The more responses, the higher the demand and the higher the rent!

So **Tip Number One** is to get a tenant who wants to be there!

Tip Number Two is to get the property recommended by a friend, an employer or a place – like a university or hospital.

What you are doing here is getting the property and the tenant more closely connected.

If the property is recommended or allocated to a tenant then they feel obliged to their employer as well as you, and so the connection is stronger. Also, if a tenant knows that you know, or are connected to, their employer in some way they are much less likely to cause you problems – just in case you go back to their boss!

Likewise, if a tenant is recommended to you from, say, a previous tenant, then the next person has an obligation to you *and* the previous tenant, and perhaps also to an employer – so the more obligations and connections you get the better, and it's always better to get a tenant through recommendation than it is to get one cold.

So the action you need to take here is to get yourself on the approved or recommended lists of as many organisations as possible – universities, employers, hospitals, councils and so on.

Tip Number Three is to attract the right tenant with your behaviour and interaction before they move in, and quality and professionalism are key here.

So make sure your adverts are good – and please make sure they are legal! You are not allowed to express any preference for race, colour, sex or creed, and please be honest in the way you describe the property and its facilities.

Overselling your property may get it filled quickly but will only lead to disappointment later on, which again leads to high turnover of tenants.

And of course, once you have attracted a selection of tenants, please make sure you take out all appropriate credit checks and references. Don't just get the address and numbers and file them – actually call the employers or the previous landlords and all referees.

I always make sure that we check a payslip or two and a couple of bank statements. By doing that you can see if a tenant is paid weekly or monthly, for example, and that may help you later with managing the ongoing tenancy.

It can be useful to use an agency here because you then have some recourse to them, as well as the tenant, if something goes wrong.

There are lots of organisations and agencies that do this for a reasonable and flat fee, so have a look on the Internet for some of those. In most cases I pass that flat fee on to the potential tenant in any case, so it doesn't have to cost anything.

Whether you do all the reference checking yourself or you use an agency – please make sure you do it!

Tip Number Four is about making sure that you control and manage the finances properly from the off, and that means getting cleared funds for both the deposit and the first month's rent before you hand over the keys. And please treat the tenant's money with care and respect and place it in a proper deposit account or insurance scheme, and in full compliance with the applicable rules and regulations.

Be clear and firm. Many tenants will try their luck here and might offer some money up front and say that they can't get it all in advance but can give you a cheque – don't do it!

As soon as you give the tenant the keys to the property you are pretty much stuck with that customer for six months so it pays to be vigilant early on – even if you relax your rules a little as the tenancy progresses.

Tip Number Five is about the legal agreements and having a full and proper Assured Shorthold Tenancy agreement properly in place before the tenant moves in.

This is actually a legal requirement and, even if you don't physically have a tenancy agreement in place, the Assured Shorthold Tenancy is considered by the law and by the courts to be in place by default should the tenancy ever get into difficulty – so you may as well get a decent agreement in place, one that protects you and the property as much as possible.

I started from the outset with a good Assured Shorthold Tenancy agreement, but as I have gone on and got more experienced I have added more and more clauses to it, and every time something went wrong, or there was a dispute, I just added another clause to the agreement to cover that specific issue.

For instance, one that caught me out in the early days was gardening. I never had a clause to say that the tenant needed to maintain the garden – but now I do!

You also might need to add specific clauses to any agreement that you use for specific properties. So, to continue on the gardening theme, for the properties in London I pay for garden refuse bins, but only if the property is in the city centre.

Start with a good agreement and enhance it as you learn, making sure that it has property-specific clauses where relevant.

Tip Number Six is to stay connected and vigilant at all times.

It's a common error for landlords to just leave the tenant alone if things appear to be going well, but a tenant can slip at any time and so I always make a point for someone in my team to keep in touch with all tenants – and to visit regularly and to respond to them.

I have a property manager and she gives her mobile phone number to all tenants, makes sure she responds to them and calls them from time to time; that way we pick up any challenges as soon as they happen and not when they have become a problem. For instance, we have one tenant who is a low-paid worker and had a friend die. Our tenant and his mates clubbed together to pay for the funeral, bless them, and consequently he couldn't pay his rent, but he told my property manager this story and we were able to adjust his rent due dates by a little bit each month and claw back the missing payments and now we're back on track. If we weren't connected to him then he might have just become a cash flow problem for the business.

Also, it makes sense to be connected to the neighbours! So we always leave a contact number with the people in the flat above or below ours, or in the house next door, and the neighbours will soon tell you if there's a problem – and then of course you can nip it in the bud.

You can hear that I believe that connection and communication is key, but that communication isn't with me personally. However, it might need to be you in the early days when you're starting off. I now have a property manager who does all of that and then pops in for a cup of tea on a Friday and tells me if there's anything I need to know or to make a decision on.

I pay that person £200 per week – it's all tax deductible – but if you don't have the spare cash for that, how about using one of your existing tenants as a communication link and perhaps knocking a few pounds off their rent? This might work if you have several properties in one location, or maybe, if you have a large HMO, one tenant in the house could communicate for all. Try that.

Tip Number Seven is about your relationship with the tenant and, for me, the key words are friendly, respectful and responsive.

I like all of my team to be friendly but never an actual friend – there's a big difference there. If you become a friend you are compromised in the business relationship, so be nice, be positive, be friendly, but stop there. And for me, that means I give a card and a cake or bottle of booze at Christmas – so a token of friendship.

The aim is for the tenant to feel that they can talk to you or one of your team if need be, so it keeps the dialogue box open and communication channels as easy as possible.

Next, please be respectful. This tenant is your customer and your cash flow – and although I wouldn't say that the customer is always right in these circumstances I would say that the customer *thinks* they're right and you have to compromise with them occasionally.

The objective is to treat this as a business relationship and with professionalism and respect, so please don't ever get personal or critical. It doesn't help, and if you do actually think that the person is a crook, then just go through the professional and legal routes to evict them rather than facing off with them – you won't ever win any conversation with aggression.

And be responsive. If you expect the tenant to pay their rent on time, they have a right to expect you to respond to them as quickly. If they have a problem, deal with it – and deal with it as quickly as you would expect a response from them. Treat them and their problems with as much care and consideration as you want you and your rent to be treated.

Stay vigilant and responsive – make sure you repair or resolve issues quickly and appropriately. Delay will not make the challenge disappear and it will annoy the tenant.

Tip Number Eight is about your business performance, and the target is to be the best landlord you can be within the circumstances of the property, and to be so good that they never want to leave.

Now here there has to be an element of going the extra mile – so if, for instance, you have a family let, make sure you let the tenant know about schools, parks, swimming pools and so on. For professional tenants, leave them the local dry cleaning collection service leaflet and so on.

Make sure you tailor information for each specific tenancy and build up a selection of information and services that are fit for purpose – maybe you even become the local collection point for the dry cleaners' pickup van. There are lots of things you can do that won't cost you any money but will make a big difference to your tenant and their decision to prefer your property over a similar one elsewhere.

I guess the focus here is to think about your tenant and their lifestyle, and think of things that make their life easier and give you and your property the edge over anything else – then your tenant will be certain that they can't live anywhere else.

Tip Number Nine is about professionalism and prudence, so get proper buildings insurance, get appropriate professional indemnity insurance and don't scrimp or cut corners on decent insurance policies.

Make sure you are an approved landlord where appropriate – whether that be an approval from the local councillor, a university or whatever. Make sure you are properly and adequately licenced if you are going to be involved with HMOs, for instance.

File everything – and make sure you keep copies of all documents; that includes copies of everything the tenant needs, as they will lose anything.

Also, keep updated – this is a serious profession and I would love it if every landlord had to be licenced, and had to keep up their professional training. I have that requirement as a chartered accountant so I don't see why professional landlords don't have the same. So be professional, businesslike and make sure you are ahead of the game in terms of rules, regulation and compliance.

My final tip, **Tip Number Ten**, is about continuing the formula. Once you have a great tenant, it's a pity if they ever leave – but if they do have to leave, the ideal scenario is that they actually find the next tenant.

If you've been a good and fair landlord then they will be happy to recommend you and your property, and again, this keeps the connection going since the new tenant then has an obligation to both you and the previous tenant.

You can always offer the old tenant some kind of incentive to do this for you as it will save you marketing and possibly agency costs – after all, if your existing tenant has stayed with you for some time they know exactly what type of tenant you are looking for and exactly the right person for the property – because it looks like them!

Finally, I just want to reiterate that all of these tips apply whether it's you, an agency or your own property manager looking after the properties – and you need to keep on top of that.

There you have it, then – the top ten tips that I stick to when dealing with tenants. The better I get at this, the fewer problems I have. I still have problem tenants from time to time, but I am much better and quicker at dealing with them than I was.

The aim for me is to get each tenant to stay for a long time and to leave only when it suits me, because that gives me the greatest level of control over my cash flow and my business and ensures that I have waiting lists of people to go into virtually all of my properties. That way, you never have to deal with voids. Try it.

Should I Let This Property Furnished or Not?

There are, in fact, three categories to consider here, which are furnished, unfurnished or part-furnished.

- Furnished means providing all the furniture required to live in the property, and there is a basic criterion for this definition, which is that the property encompasses the necessary furniture to enable a person to eat, sleep and sit within the property.

- Unfurnished is, of course, the exact opposite, where nothing is provided and the tenant furnishes the property themselves.

- Part-furnished means a middle ground where you provide curtains, carpets and generally the white goods: fridge, cooker and washing machine. This means that the tenant needs only to provide what they need in addition to this. The advantage here is that it is clearly cheaper for you when you set up the property.

The decision about whether to furnish or not is made mainly from the type of tenancy you provide. So, if you provide *accommodation* for people, you need to provide furniture. Accommodation is normally provided, for instance, if you have student lets, sharers, or corporate lets. In this case you will have more chance of finding a tenant and getting a decent rent, as these groups of people tend not to have their own furniture. In most other cases furniture is not necessary or required as other groups of people are more likely to have their own furniture, or to want to furnish to their own taste and standards.

Points to note:

- Whatever furniture you provide at the beginning of the tenancy, and include in the tenancy agreement or the inventory, you need to continue to provide, and in the equivalent condition, throughout the tenancy period.

- Be careful with the safety aspects of the furniture – look up the latest criteria on the web.

- You can hire the entire furniture contents of a property – and that hire charge is also tax deductible.

- If the tenant provides the furniture then they should insure it, but if you provide the furniture it is likely that you should insure it, unless you have a specific clause in your tenancy agreements for the tenant to insure furniture.

Final Amazing Point About Income Strategies

This is the last point I want to make about financials and income strategies and it's a whopper, so listen up!

If we go back to our Wash its Face calculation again and look at the components:

- Rent
- Funding Costs
- Insurances
- Management Fees
- Gas and Safety Checks
- Other Costs

Now, these aren't the only components – your Wash its Face may have all sorts of stuff in there that I haven't included here – but let's just use what we have to make this point.

Let's assume we're looking at buying an investment property – we haven't bought it yet and we're still debating. We've run the numbers, it's cash positive and the ROCI is acceptable.

Now look at it again:

The rent – we can find out exactly how much rent we can get with 100% certainty by finding a tenant before we buy, either through a local newspaper ad or another way. We could even get a tenancy agreement signed.

The funding costs we can find out with 100% certainty, and we could even get a mortgage in principle, which would tell us the exact amount to the penny we would need to pay out each month.

We can get an insurance quote for the property; we could get a quote for management fees and even sign the contract there; we could get a quote for the gas safety checks and any other costs we want to include.

So before we even buy the property we can know what our cash flow and our return are going to be. Furthermore, we know what those figures are going to be for at least the next six months because we could have a six-month tenancy agreement (an Assured Shorthold Tenancy agreement).

Therefore we could start this property investing business with **100% certainty** of our short-term financial future – now what other business can you start that does that?

If you want to open a shop, or start a plumbing or a coaching business, you can estimate what your cash flow might be given certain assumptions but you can never be absolutely confident what those numbers are going to be – with a property investing business you can!

I don't like risk – I'm a chartered accountant by training and naturally cautious. I'm a widowed mother of three children and can't afford to take risks with my money, and their inheritance. So that's why I like property – because done **properly** and **professionally** it gives me **certainty**, it's **predictable** and it gives me **security**.

Action Plan

CHAPTER 5

Investing For Capital Appreciation

Buying a property with the intention to generate a capital gain is a completely different strategy to the income one we've been through, but sadly the inexperienced person doesn't really understand that because the properties can look very similar.

With an income property, you are aiming at a regular dose of cash flow so that you can use that to pay your own living costs, whereas the property bought for capital growth is bought with the intention of creating a big lump of cash at some stage.

Broadly, there are two types of capital strategy and I call those Buff and Fluff (B&F) and Capital Projects (CP).

A B&F property is one that needs just that – a good clean, a lick of paint, another clean and out it goes. So it's a cosmetically distressed property only. A CP is where a property needs much more attention: a new roof, a new bathroom, plumbing replaced and so on.

What Distinguishes Different Capital Strategies?

My rule of thumb on all these capital strategies is this: if it's a property that my family and I could probably do up given time and a prevailing wind, then that's a B&F.

Secondly, if it's a property that has got bits missing – like a window or a door – that's a CP and needs expert help.

Thirdly, if it's a property that has got big bits bit missing, like a whole wall or a roof or a floor somewhere, or the property itself is sloping, damaged or cracked, then that's a structural deal and I personally wouldn't do it unless I had a structural person on my team.

So, done properly, property investing can provide regular smaller lumps of cash for your day-to-day requirements from the income properties, plus bigger dollops of cash when needed, for, say, a wedding or university or retirement from the capital ones.

The professional makes sure that they have both types, and we cover that in the strategic section, but if we look now at capital gain we have one principle, and that is to make more money from the property than would be made purely from natural market movements.

Now, you could be satisfied with making the money that the market movements naturally make – our 10% or 16% per year that we identified earlier – but that's not really professional investing. Any idiot can sit on their backside and let the market move; but of course, if you are going to do that then you have to be prepared for the market to also go down. The professional investor protects themselves by buying properties that are more likely to go up irrespective of the market – now that's less risky and more profitable than the 'just sitting on your bum' approach.

So our principle is to find properties that are more likely to go up, and more quickly than normal.

Locating the Perfect Property for Capital Appreciation

Now, we know that the aim here is to find a property that will increase in value more quickly than the general market and over the last thirty-odd years I have developed a technique for spotting those; as usual, I have turned that into a mnemonic.

I first wrote this in about 1983 when I was trying to work out why my first property had risen so much and, over the years, I have expanded this to incorporate *every single reason* why a property can outperform the market: the property itself, the location, the method of sale and marketplace, the owner and the transaction method.

The mnemonic is **UPWARDS**, and that may be familiar to you if you have attended any property education seminars or networks because, I'm delighted to say, this process has become the industry standard for assessing this type of property.

So, from the horse's mouth, then, what do we look for?

UPWARDS

The **U** in **UPWARDS** stands for *up and coming*, and the point here is to find a property that is going to ride a strong up-market movement because it's in an up and coming area of some kind. Now this means that the area isn't already 'up' in the first place – so what you are looking for here are areas that are currently not popular.

This was my very first investing lesson as I bought my first property in 1977 with the intention of providing myself with accommodation so that I could go to university – or to provide me with a rental income to pay for what I saw at the time as the extortionate price of university accommodation.

I got a place at Sussex University, just outside of Brighton, and I scurried down there beforehand to have a look at the flats there. I discovered that they were well out of my price range – even then Brighton was a fashionable place to live and prices were always high. So I went home and drove back to London up the A23, passing a place called Burgess Hill, which is about eleven miles north of Brighton. I discovered that I could buy a proper family three-bedroom house there for the price of a tiny flat in Brighton, so that's exactly what I did: I bought a three-bed semi there for just under £7,500.

I left university three years later and sold that house for nearly £30k, quadrupling my money. Even then that was one hell of a return, and the reason was that, despite my ignorance, I had bought in an area which was just about to have a massive uplift due mainly to the train connections as Burgess Hill gradually became a London commuter town – and that happened because the properties in towns further north, like Haywards Heath, had become too expensive.

This was a big learning experience for me.

By accident, I had fallen upon a real up and coming area. I liked that, and wanted to do it again, so I sat and thought about all the components that I had hit upon.

Not only was there the train line to London but the town was developing – there was even some light industry to the edge of town, good schools and good road links both south, to Brighton, and north, to London. Businesses were moving into the town and a new sports hall was being built.

Added to all of that, I also realised that part of the gain in the value of that property happened because of the ripple, or knock-on effect, of Burgess Hill's proximity to a high-priced area, Haywards Heath.

Another example of the ripple effect is in east London. I was born in West Ham but if I wanted to sell my house for more money I would tell people it was in Stratford, because people have heard more about Stratford and think of it as a good place, whereas West Ham has less of a positive reputation. Now West Ham and Stratford are one and the same place and linked by one road (West Ham Lane) a few hundred yards long, but the difference in property prices will be marked.

So, the professional investor will always choose the poor end of the street because that's most likely to be up and coming. The streets just alongside a posh or high-priced area will always be the up and coming ones; the properties in an area where there are communication developments, like new roads, airport development or rail links, will always be up and coming. Properties close to retail, recreational, leisure or educational developments will always be up and coming. All of these are great reasons for an area to have that lovely kick up in prices.

One other example of this is the recent rise in prices in Manchester. There were obvious signs of a rise in prices coming – due partly to the £80 million Manchester Airport development. All the UPWARD signs were there during middle and late 2013 and Manchester then closed the year with a 21% increase in property prices.

So for the **U** in **UPWARDS**, deliberately look for areas just outside the high-priced zones; look for properties in areas where development will take place in the future as they will give you the biggest profit.

As a tip, often the local UDP – or Unitary Development Plan – will detail future plans for an area, so go on to the web and search for them.

The **P** in **UPWARDS** stands for property *potential* and, funnily enough, I have always viewed any investment property as a piece of play-dough: flexible and pliable and ready to be moulded into something. When I look at a property, I think about how I could change it to create more money. Now this is not the same as looking at a property and thinking of colour schemes or décor – I don't have that kind of vision – but I am able to see if a property has potential to be turned into a different and more profitable unit.

Look at a property and see if it could be extended or changed around – could it have an attic conversion or a garage added, and would any of those things actually increase the value?

Try and see any property as just a footprint and a blank canvas – try not to fall in love with it as it is – and what you are looking for is the best possible and most profitable use of the property outline or footprint.

Often you can get a better idea of a property's potential by looking at the aerial view, which is easy to do on the web.

I did that when I first looked at the property I shall call 'Charlie's House'. Before I actually completed on buying that house I looked at the aerial view and noticed that it looked out of balance and that, from the air, the house looked a bit like a letter Z that hadn't been finished off; the bottom leg or strut of the Z was missing.

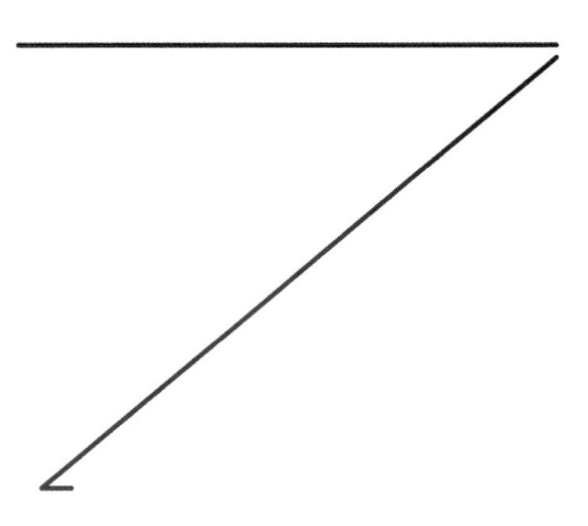

I immediately put in planning permission to add that bottom strut as an extension to balance the property up. Now from the ground the imbalance wasn't noticeable, but I saw the possibility from the aerial view.

In addition, I noticed that all the local gardens were quite small and yet the garden of Charlie's House was large – and had enough room to put a spare house in the garden without making the original garden too small in comparison to the others around it.

So I applied for planning permission for that too.

Then finally, I thought that if the house was extended, to add the bottom part of the letter Z, it would definitely make it the biggest and grandest in the village and therefore maybe a bit too big – so I also came up with a plan to split the house into three smaller terraced houses – and I got planning permission for that too.

So, by the time I had actually completed on the house, I had three separate planning permissions on it to do different things depending on how I wanted to develop the potential of the house and its footprint.

By the way – as in this case – you don't have to own a house to apply for planning permission on it. So get used to spotting and playing about with a property's fuller potential – and that is best spotted when you first look at it. Once you've had a house for a while, you can't actually see it in a different way, so add a point to your property viewing checklists to look for opportunities when you first view.

The final thing to say here is don't get too tied to properties that already look like houses – spot the potential in empty churches, police stations, school buildings or farm buildings for instance. Also, remember that an investment property doesn't necessarily even need to have four walls, and we could be looking at the potential in a lighthouse or windmill.

The principle to remember is that an investment property is purely a cash-generating vehicle and nothing else. Get used to changing your perspective and seeing the world through a different lens.

The **W** in **UPWARDS** stands for something that is wrong, and initially, I never believed that anybody got anything *wrong* – I believed in the honesty of the estate agent and the vendors and I believed in the purity of the purchaser – but now I'm older and wiser and I know for sure that most people in the property game get most things wrong most of the time.

And that's a vanity thing. Most people want to believe that their house is worth more than it is because it makes them feel good.

Sellers also suffer from vanity when they choose an estate agent – the snob in all of us wants to use the upmarket estate agent, when actually a lower-profiled agent that sells flats may be better suited to the property we have.

If we choose the wrong agent, the agent will undervalue it – and agents value properties wrongly all the time! Sometimes it's deliberate – they don't want a particular property in their window, so they undervalue it to get it sold quickly – and sometimes it's just an error. And do bear in mind that many estate agents aren't investors and may have no concept of what a property might be worth.

I have two big HMOs which were undervalued by about £50–75k each purely because the agent had no idea of what an HMO was or what the income potential was – he simply saw the houses as domestic dwellings broken into cumbersome and troublesome sets of rooms; consequently he valued them completely wrong. The properties weren't familiar to him, and they would have been a problem for him personally, so he made an assumption that they were problematic for all.

So, the trick here is to learn your specialism well. If you like one-bedroom flats, for example, then learn the value of every single one and all the standard variants; then you'll be able to outthink and outvalue any agent or seller, and pick the ones that work for you.

Have confidence in your own judgement. You have a strong motivation to value things properly – agents don't.

Now, the **A** stands for *alternative markets*, and I will include in this section any alternative market outlets, including auctions, where property is transacted outside of the normal estate agent in the high street.

The reason this category often leads to a quick uplift in value is because transacting outside of agencies saves money and you can often get these properties cheap.

If we look at auctions for instance, what the seller is generally looking for is a quick deal. Most auction properties, if sold on the day, are exchanged on that day and completed within twenty-eight days – so the seller knows for certain that if there's a buyer in the room, they will have their cash in a month.

The timing isn't as certain if you sell through an agent and, at the time of writing, a property takes an average of *twenty weeks* to complete – so a person selling at the auction swaps that time certainty for a discount on the price. Also, of course, there's no estate agent's fee to pay; there will be an auction house fee but that tends to be less.

Auctions are great fun and I recommend that everybody pop into their local auction from time to time. It also provides local knowledge as that's where the local investors will hang out, and it gives a perspective on local prices and properties available.

However, buying or selling at an auction takes skill and experience; the novice trader will generally suffer here at the hands of both the local expert property traders *and* the auctioneer, so make sure you do your homework and visit any auction several times before you actually buy or sell there as it will give you a sense of where properties are priced, and also give you some steer on the behaviour of the specific auctioneer. Each auction can be quite different in character and process, so if you are not aware of all of that you may lose out.

In summary, then – caution with auctions.

The **R** stands for a *radical or revolutionary transaction method*, and I always quickly run my eye over this every time I evaluate a property because I want to explore the possibilities of transacting the property in a different or unusual way.

The obvious one here is to buy the property using a lease option. I could buy a property on a lease option, which means that I might pay a monthly premium for a short period of time, but what I am actually purchasing – rather than the property itself – is an option to purchase in the future. And I can buy or sell properties this way.

This is unusual or radical because it's not the standard method of transacting, where we exchange and complete over a given period of about a month.

Also, I may never actually own the property so clearly that's not a normal transaction.

These radical transactions or purchasing methods come and go and one I used a lot in the past was a reversionary contract. This isn't used nowadays but was a sale and leaseback contract, which is more commonly used nowadays in commercial property transactions.

So these radical purchasing or transaction methods change with time and no doubt there will be another one along soon, and it's worth keeping them in mind as it may enable you to purchase or profit from property by being knowledgeable and smart rather than using plain old-fashioned cash and ownership.

The **D** in **UPWARDS** stands for *distressed property*, and to find these just ask yourself the basic question: – is it ugly?

Quite often a property looks ugly. It may have brown swirly 1960s carpets, or an out-of-date bathroom suite, or bright pink walls. In most cases, all the property needs is a damn good clean and a quick paint (generally with a neutral colour) from top to bottom.

As mentioned previously, I call these B&Fs because what they need more than anything is a bit of elbow grease, spit and polish.

Some people call these cosmetically distressed properties, but that's not a good enough term for these B&Fs as all distressed properties – whether these, with just surface problems, or the more problematic and structurally distressed – are cosmetically challenged, so we need to differentiate between those two extremes.

Generally, for it to be just a B&F it will be either:

- **Old-fashioned and in need of updating.**
- **One of those properties with unusual decoration.**

Or in some cases, if a property has been stuck on the market for a while, what often helps is a massive clean (and then another clean), a de-clutter of stuff and maybe a quick lick of paint.

Be careful that you concentrate here with looking at properties with surface distress only: you want it ugly, not derelict. That includes properties that need a lick of paint, or a new bathroom or kitchen, or maybe a complete redecoration inside and out, but never a property that has structural problems, or planning problems or structural engineering problems.

Yes, those are still distressed, but in a different way as they are likely to need renovating, which would be a bigger job involving replacing bathrooms, kitchens, electrics, plumbing, and maybe repairing the roof, foundations or other external features. With these projects you would almost certainly need a professional and qualified building team – and that would move the properties into either the CP tier of our portfolio or the **Fancy Pants Deal (FPD)** arena – all good projects, but not the simple B&F type.

Distressed Properties to Consider:

- Properties that have not kept pace with fashion or trend. People's needs are always changing and here we need to look at not only those properties that are out of date in terms of décor, but also those that no longer reflect changing lifestyles. For instance, years ago it was usual to have a house with only one bathroom, but nowadays, most houses would have more than that; main bedrooms in modern-built houses almost always have an en-suite facility, and many properties would have a bathroom for every two bedrooms.

- Property built in the 1900s, which means property up to a hundred years old, or possibly a little older. The Victorian era is reputed to be a great one for building so anything built then – say, from 1880 onwards – would be great. They are solid and have stood the test of time, but often need updating. Very modern properties rarely need much work done on them, so look for properties built between 1880 and 1980!

- Property that is conventionally built of brick with a tile or slate roof is best because you know that you are dealing with standard materials in a standard way.

- Refurbishments which deal with unusual materials, say, wood, stone or concrete, present their own problems in that not every finance house will provide loans on them and not all builders work with them – so don't make things too difficult for yourself and stick to the ordinary stuff. It goes without saying that odd roofs, such as thatch, are incredibly hard to work with and thatchers are in such short supply that at the moment you would have to wait about two years to get your roof done – during which time all your profits disappear.

- Property that you could live in – just! If the property is totally uninhabitable then it is likely that it's a specialist project.

- Empty homes. If a property is empty, always try and ask, or work out, why that is – it could be because, say, an owner has died, but it could also be because the plumbing doesn't work, the roof leaks and there is no heating. Be especially careful here to identify problems that are not always readily apparent, like rot or damp.

- Properties that are out of kilter with their surroundings, in terms of condition or quality, because it is then an easy task to bring the property up to standard, and the surrounding houses give us the template of how it should look when finished.

So, in summary then, the ideal property for a distressed project is probably one of the following:

- Victorian or Edwardian.

- Thirty to forty years old and past their prime, out of their guarantee period and showing signs of wear. These are generally decorated in orange and brown with an avocado-coloured bathroom!

- Any other property that has just not been maintained well, and may be dirty and unkempt.

As you can hear, the term 'distressed' covers a lot of different properties, but if you start with the premise 'Is it ugly in some way?' you will quickly learn to spot them.

And finally in **UPWARDS** we have the **S**, which stands for the *seller is motivated* to sell. Before I list some examples here, I need to say that you may never really know exactly why a seller is motivated to sell, and sell cheap.

There may be some deep-rooted emotional reason involved which they will never reveal, and so you need to learn to turn your emotional side off. Often when I tell people about deals where it's been a particularly good deal for me they say, "Why would the seller sell that if they knew the price of comparative properties?"

And in all honesty, in many cases I have absolutely no idea – I would go mad trying to understand why humans act the way they do, because in the main the reasons are totally bizarre, so I have learned to just evaluate my deal, put in an offer and accept it – if they do.

Having said all that, there tends to be three main reasons:

- Change of life circumstances, and in this category I would put divorce and separation; or change in family structure, so more children coming or children leaving, or maybe an older parent needing to move in. So any circumstance where the property is no longer suitable for the way of life of the owner or owners is one grouping. In these cases, the emotional pressure of the older parent, or the empty nest syndrome, pushes to the front of the queue in terms of the seller's motivation and, consequently, they accept a lower price in return for emotional certainty in the circumstance.

- Change of financial circumstances – so loss of a job or gaining of promotion; receipt of a whacking bonus or being made redundant; or the owner may just work for IBM, which I think stands for I Be Moving – so the job they have could require them to move regularly to different places.

In those circumstances, the owners just have to move and, in many cases, they exchange price for speed and, particularly if their employer is paying relocation fees, the price they get for the property ceases to be as important. And finally:

- Death of the owner or one of the owners, which is a pretty final event. And here the property then becomes completely different in that it will either become a millstone round the neck of the remaining owner, or it may just become a surplus asset in the cases of estate sales.

Imagine you are a beneficiary of your Auntie Flo's will and finally Auntie Flo dies and you know you have been left a property or a share of one. At that stage it's all bonus because one day you didn't have the property and now you do – and with these executor sales the price is normally the least important thing; in those cases the beneficiaries just want to sell the property and get spending with their inheritance.

So, in all three categories of motivated seller, what you, as the purchaser, provide is speed, certainty and, in many cases, solutions to problems, and if you concentrate on that then you will get some good financial deals in return.

There we have it, then – the full range of **UPWARDS**. Get used to running that mnemonic through your head every time you look at a property – it will be worth the effort and you will get quicker and better at spotting the deals that work.

And it doesn't matter which order you spot them in as **UPWARDS** can be used in any order; the letters just represent the seven reasons why a property will go up in value more quickly than, or in excess of, the average or standard property market growth.

And importantly, **UPWARDS** is a cumulative thing. If you find a property that has one of the capital growth identifiers then you have a property with a good prospect of a strong capital gain – but if you find a property with two of the identifiers or characteristics, then the growth is likely to be greater and so on. The most identifiers I have ever had in one single property is probably just about four and a half, and I have found properties with four of the identifiers a couple of times and they have all been big profit generators.

However, finding those would be unusual – certainly for a novice or inexperienced investor – so maybe build up to that over time.

Evaluation for Capital Strategies

Calculating our return on capital strategies is very easy, so when I am assessing any project I do the following:

- Get an estimate of what the property will be worth once it's finished. Sometime this is very easy as there are lots of other similar properties for sale and you can check some comparables. However, sometimes it's more complicated and you have to pay for an external valuation or estimate.
  Obviously, for smaller individual properties you can take valuations from the web using your own judgement, but if you are doing a larger CP or an FPD here then make sure you are absolutely sure of your end value before you start or part with any money.
- Deduct from that the cost of original purchase.
- Also deduct the cost of renovation or development or whatever you're doing.
- Deduct the cost of borrowing, if any, to buy this property.
- Deduct a provision for selling costs or agents' fees.
- Allow something for your own time, or a project manager's time if you are using one.
- Allow a general contingency for the unexpected.
- Deduct all of that from your estimated sales price to get an overall profit.
- Then calculate your profit percentage by dividing the profit by the total costs and multiplying by 100 – and there you are.

Don't forget that this percentage profit may be for any length of time, so you can then adjust it to arrive at an annual percentage figure to give yourself a return on investment (ROCI) figure that you can then compare to others.

Return for CPs

I have worked out, over forty years of doing these projects, that my general estimated rate of return is 10% per strand of UPWARDS.

So, if the property is in an up and coming area, I reckon I can make 10% on that; if it's also distressed that makes another 10%, so 20% in total, and if the seller is motivated to sell I add another 10% to get 30% and so on.

It's a simple but effective quick assessment guide.

Illustration

Let's say I see an advertisement in the local post office window offering a house for sale at £78,000. The property is distressed when I see it and I agree to buy it for £72,000 from the seller, who is motivated following separation from his wife. I estimate that the property needs £5,000 of work on it, the project needs about three months to complete and, once done, the property will be worth £125,000.

For simplicity, I'm going to assume that I can borrow all of the money to do this at 5% per annum, and that I can borrow the money I need for exactly the length of the project.

Stage One

I look at the property and circumstantial details and quickly run them through **UPWARDS**.

I get four 'ticks':

- ☐ **It has Potential.**
- ☐ **The sale is advertised in the Wrong place (local post office!).**
- ☐ **The property is Distressed.**
- ☐ **The seller is motivated.**

Now, on a rough guess, if I can make 40% (four times the 10% per tick guideline) it's worth me going through the detailed numbers as above:

Stage Two

Eventual sales price	£125,000
Less: purchase price	£72,000
Less: project costs	£5,000
Less: cost of borrowing £75,000	
(our simple 5% pa for three months)	£938
Initial profit	**£47,062**
Less:	
Sales costs – say 1% of sales price	£1,250
Less: contingency – say 10% of project cost	£500
Adjusted profit	**£45,312**

Stage Three

I then calculate my expected rate of return on my cash by adding up all of the costs first:

£72,000 + £5,000 + £1,250 + £500 + £938 = £79,688

Then calculating the percentage return as follows:

£45,312/£79,688 x 100 = 56.8%

Stage Four

I then take that and add in the duration or time factor. This project is expected to be done in three months so, in theory, that would mean we could multiply this 56.8% by four to get an annual return – that would be a whopping 227%.

Stage Five

I then do a sanity check and look at what that all means, and make sure it all works. My initial guess was that it should make me 40% profit. The detail tells me that it's likely to be nearer 56.8%, and that there's also a spare £45,312 of cash in the deal to pay me for my time in the project.

Example Strategy: Timing

A Professional's **UPWARDS** Strategy: Timing the Transaction. When summer starts to fade and I see leaves falling I start looking for B&F bargains. I move into B&Fs in the autumn for two main reasons: firstly, the market traditionally starts to cool about then, so people who have had their property on the market for a while start to drop their prices. They know that the property market is about to slow over the winter and suddenly they are facing the possibility of no sale for a few months.

Unless the property is pristine, then almost any place could do with a lick of paint and a decent clean, which is basically all a B&F needs.

To pick up these properties, my ideal target is to complete the purchase before Christmas Eve, so I start looking to exchange in October or early November with a December completion.

Then, once you have it, you have about a month to tart it up before the January market opens. In January, many people get that sense of wanting to start a new year with a clean start, and so this is a very popular time for people to start renting – after all, many of them have been cooped up all Christmas with their families so they're desperate to get out!

So, clearly my intention is to rent it almost immediately after it's been buffed, and that would be in January the following year. However, if it doesn't rent for any reason I have a contingency to resell it – I am close then to the spring bounce time when, traditionally, property rises a bit. So, if I do have to sell I don't have to hold on to it for too long before I should find a buyer.

Again, human beings normally start their DIY at about Easter, and they tend to get their itchy feet at about the same time and think about moving. So late March, early April is a perfect time to put a property on the market to sell.

Added to that of course is that if you can complete before the 5th April you'll be able to use your capital gains tax allowance for the year in question, which tends to get lost for most people. At the time of writing the annual exempt amount is £11,100 per person.

The second reason I move into B&Fs in the autumn is that suddenly you get a lot of builders and their power teams wanting to come and work inside rather than being out in the cold – poor things. I actually know an investor that finds projects for his teams to do overseas in the winter and then brings them back to the UK for our summer.

Anyway, you do get a lot more builders available in the winter as they all want to come inside if they can – and that's partly so that they can keep working and earning rather than losing days to ice or snow. This means that you can be a bit more aggressive with your price negotiations with them, particularly if heating is included.

Going into B&Fs in the autumn takes advantage of all of those natural and normal market rhythms and movements.

Getting Started with Capital

Before you get started you need to do a lot of planning, and this time spent at the beginning will save a lot of time during the project – and we know that speed is of the essence.

Firstly, you need to decide your own level of involvement. Are you going to be the one-man band redecoration expert doing this in your spare time, or are you going to be completely hands-off and employ all the manpower you need from outside? The main approaches are:

- To do it all yourself.
- To manage it yourself with external contractors.
- To outsource all the activity to others.

And there are benefits to each approach. However, be clear before you start what it is you are doing, and don't overestimate your own time and ability or underestimate your contractors. There is nothing worse for a contractor than being constantly interrupted by an owner who thinks they know best! So you need to decide how involved you are going to be. Ask yourself:

- Do you enjoy DIY?
- Do you have spare time?
- Is the refurbishment simple?

If you can answer yes to all three, then consider doing the job yourself, or, if you lack certain skills, time or energy, allow somebody else to do the work for you.

I always say that as you get more experienced in property your definition of DIY changes. In the early days, DIY stands for Do It Yourself, but by the time you've been at this a while, your definition of DIY might change to Don't Involve Yourself!

Decide what works for you, and if you want to have a go yourself then what better autumn and winter hobby could there be than redecorating one of your properties? It gives you something to do in the long evenings, I reckon – and then you can go out and party in the summer. Whoever's going to do the work, we still need a plan. This should cover:

- All the jobs that need doing.
- What skill is needed; e.g. carpentry, decorating, gardening.
- An estimate of the overall time needed and cost.
- The order in which the tasks need doing.
- The estimated timings for each part of the project.

If you are going to do all the work yourself don't forget to include a cost for your own time – say, £25 per hour, or whatever you believe you are worth – as this often concentrates the mind.

Then you can start the redecoration, and here make sure that you have a systematic approach. So either start at the back of the house and work your way to the front or vice versa. And always start at the top of the house and work down.

Likewise, in each individual room start at the top with the ceilings and then work your way down the walls to the floor. Then go through with finishing, or dressing of the property as the last action inside.

There we have it, then: a simple capital strategy taking advantage of natural market rhythms combined with **UPWARDS**.

Checklist – download copies of this from www.fieldingfinancial.com.

- ☐ **U**p and coming
- ☐ **P**otential for development
- ☐ **W**rong marketplace or price
- ☐ **A**lternative marketplace and auctions
- ☐ **R**adical transaction method
- ☐ **D**istressed property
- ☐ **S**eller motivated to sell

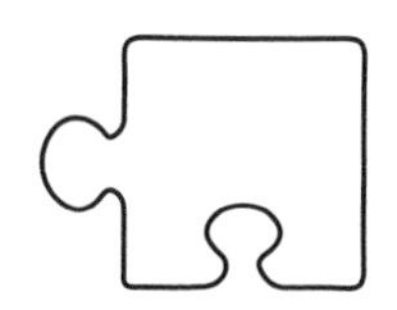

CHAPTER 6

Strategic Planning

Introduction to Strategy

Many people who fall into property investing are dream-seekers.

They are the people who watch all the property programmes on the telly and get sucked in by the entertainment value – but be warned: they are only entertainment programmes and not property investment programmes. You can't put investment programmes on the telly without the TV company being sued for giving advice, so they are *not* investment education programmes.

Then, after the dream-seekers we have the accidental landlords who find themselves with a property for one of several reasons:

- Their aged, dotty aunt dies and leaves them a flat in Worthing.
- They want to move and can't sell their flat so they rent it out and move on.
- They set up home with someone and have a spare property between them, so one gets rented out.

Let's be very clear – none of this is property investing! It isn't even the start of property investing and you shouldn't be deluded into thinking it is – otherwise this dreaming or accidental property will become a nightmare for you.

However, the accidental property *could* be the start of a portfolio if you're prepared to work at it, get educated, get some experience, get in with a good, knowledgeable support group – and add to the portfolio quickly.

What is needed to start to move from the accidental activity to the professional investor is a business plan and a strategy.

Now that sounds a bit grander than it needs to be, but we must have some concept of this as we go forward.

Incidentally, there is currently some discussion going on in Europe about investment funding, whereby accidental landlords will *not* be able to get investment-type funding and professionals will. Their distinction between the two is based on the existence or absence of a plan or strategy, so even the European Union understand that this is the fundamental point.

Portfolio Structure

So the first issue we need to address is size – and size is (in this case anyway) important.

Because one property, or even two, or three, or five isn't a portfolio – and it doesn't constitute professional property investing. It's the start of a portfolio, but only that.

We want nineteen!

The Perfect Pyramid Portfolio

For any would-be property investor, I think it's worth identifying what sort of properties stand the test of time, and if we look around the world there is one structure that still stands after thousands of years – a pyramid. There's a good reason for that: it's structurally sound with great foundations; it's made of the right materials; it doesn't overload the top and it's built on the standard Fibonacci expansion ratio – or the Golden Mean.

Now, if you don't know about Fibonacci then look him up on the web - but to cut it short, Fibonacci discovered that nature expands at a given rate, and that holds true for shells, trees, rabbits and even the universe. Leonardo da Vinci took it one stage further and discovered that we consider people beautiful if they are 'structured' along this standard ratio, and in our modern financial life the ratio is used as an investment strategy, as a determinant for financial products (even a credit card fits this same 'right' size), and it is even used in branding (the Apple logo for instance).

The theory is this: if this pattern is omnipresent in nature, then it's present in the financial world, or at least, it's present in the factors that make up finances, like market psychology and economic patterns. The ratio is 1:1.62, and the standard rate of growth is 0,1,2,3,5,8, and so on, with each number being the sum of the previous two. OK, lesson over.

So, when we look at property investing today it makes sense to utilise this knowledge, and we can create the perfect property portfolio, or property pyramid, using all this evidence, information and structure.

That's why we start with a pyramid in our property trainings, and we divide the pyramid into a standard property portfolio with investments in:

- **BTLs**: Buy-to-let properties (the simple lower-risk lettings), and then we move up through
- **B&Fs**: Buff and Fluff (simple cosmetic refurbishments), to
- **HMOs**: Houses of Multiple Occupation and higher risk rentals; then to
- **CPs**: Capital Refurbishments, and then to the top of the risk profile to the
- **FPDs**: Fancy Pants Deals which would be anything tricky, complicated or risky.

Now, if we take this profile from high-risk down to low-risk investments, and add the potential number of properties to it on each level, based on the Fibonacci sequence, our standard pyramid looks like this:

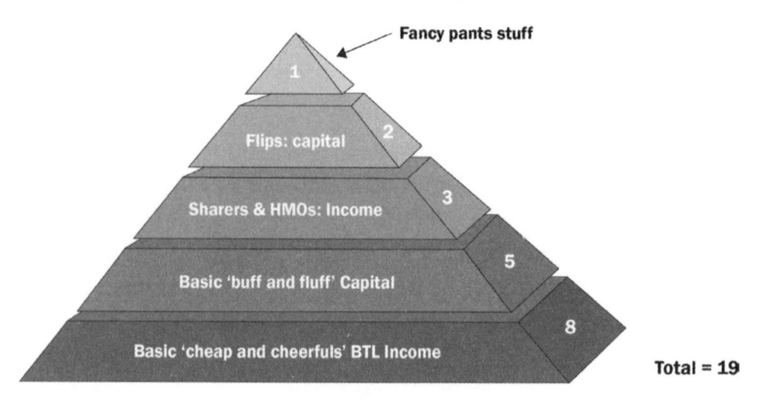

So the 'perfect' property portfolio, or pyramid, consists of:

- 1 Fancy Pants Deal (FPD).
- 2 Higher-end (CPs).

- 3 HMOs (HMO).
- 5 Buff and Fluffs (B&F).
- 8 Buy-to-lets (BTL).

This is a total of nineteen properties covering all risk levels, all disciplines and time scales and all income levels.

Risk

It is important that you understand the concept of risk and where it occurs. The least problematic and challenging investment is one that is:

- Small.
- Generates income to cover the costs.
- Carries minimal inherent risk.

And if you add those three criteria together you get a simple buy-to-let property. They tend to be smaller (one- or two-bedroom flats or small houses), and if you follow the formulas they will bring cash flow each month and they carry less inherent risk than the other types of property.

Although there are things that can go wrong with BTL, their impact is relatively small. If you lose a tenant, well, it tends not to break you financially if you have to pay for it for a month or so; and, as the property is relatively small, the cost of any repairs or maintenance tends to be containable (or doable by yourself).

And that's why *most* people start with a buy-to-let property, and why they form the base of our pyramid. They are the foundation stones and the ballast in our portfolio.

You won't go broke having a series of BTLs and banking cheques every month but, conversely, they are unlikely to make you terribly rich or financially free because they are small and they just don't generate enough money on their own.

At this stage, some amateur investors make the decision to just get more BTLs, so that they can build up their income into a sizeable amount just from volume, but that in itself can be risky.

If you have only one type of investment and something affects that – for instance, let's say the next government brings in landlord registration for buy-to-let properties which, for some reason, you can't get – your property business is now stuck and your income potentially gone.

So it's also risky to have too many of any one thing.

And in any case, after a few BTLs most professionals get the urge for some HMOs, where the income tends to be much higher and the returns for your efforts and money are far greater.

But conversely, going up to HMOs may also carry more risk. The amount of money involved is larger, there are more people in one house and who are more likely to be causing damage and you have to get licenced.

Also, most lenders won't lend for HMO purchases to investors unless the investor already has some existing experience (for instance the lender will ask if they have, say, six months' landlord experience and at least one other property), but each lender is different so please check with the broker for exact conditions.

Then, when we look at capital strategies, we need some small ones that we can do and that don't take up much money (B&F) and some larger ones that generate bigger lumps of cash (CPs).

Finally, once we have the first four tiers of the portfolio under control and we're safely paying our way each month, then we add a bit of spice to the portfolio and get access to a FPD.

Now I say 'get access to' deliberately there because most people don't go to those projects on their own as they will often be big (say, a housing estate development) or difficult (say, requiring extensive planning permission, or an expert or specialist or both).

You can do those yourself but at Fielding Financial we take the approach of doing some of these FPDs as joint ventures between all of our customers, trainers, mentors and me, so that we spread the risk – and the excitement! We find these deals and offer them to all, and all our connected people can participate as little or as much as they want to.

Strategic Summary

On balance we need little bits of income, bigger bits of income – all paying money on a monthly basis – which we can use to feed the family and pay the gas bill, *plus* lumps of cash and larger lumps of cash periodically to pay for the larger expenses in life: weddings, holidays and cars, etc.

In addition, we all need some money now and some in the future, so we need to be setting up deals that will mature and pay out in the months and years to come. But we need balance and to protect ourselves, and the pyramid approach to a property portfolio is the best way to provide all that in one structure that I have found in forty years of investing.

Experienced Investor's Tip

We all understand that the more we know about a topic, the less risk there is.

When you can't drive, to get into a car and move it is a risky business but, after we have learned how to do it and have had a few years' experience, most of us drive on an 'automatic pilot' basis most of the time.

The same is true for property investing: the more you know and the more educated you get, the less risk you take. Also, professionals get themselves connected to a relevant group of experts and other investors.

So, to reduce your risk, get educated - constantly, as this field is always changing - and get connected!

Setting a Strategic Plan

Income

Let's look at income first because we need to generate income from this so that we can be financially free, and then we can have freedom of life choice.

Using standard or average expected returns for the two income-generating levels of the pyramid – HMOs (where we should get at least £1k per month after costs per property) and BTL (where we should get at least £100 per month after costs per property) – our potential monthly income from the pyramid is:

HMOs: £1k x 3 properties =	£3,000
Plus:	
BTL: £100 x 8 properties =	£800
Total income	**£3,800**

Which is perfect because the average monthly cost of running a household in the UK, at £1,900, is half that generated by the standard pyramid.

And this creates the ideal financial balance: half of the money generated by the property portfolio goes towards living now and feeding the kids and the cat, and the other half generated goes towards the future and could be reinvested in the next project.

Individual Strategy

We can also work this backwards. Let's say your specific living requirements are for £3,000 per month.

Take that figure and double it (maintaining the half now and half future ratio) to set your monthly target of £6,000 to be generated from the property pyramid.

To generate £6,000 per month we know that we can either invest in six HMOs (at £1,000 per month) or sixty BTLs (at £100 per month). We probably wouldn't want either of these extremes so we create a balance based on our experience, required risk level, and knowledge.

So we can then work around the options and we could have four HMOs (£4,000 per month), and then add twenty BTLs (£2,000) to that, or go for five HMOs (£5,000) and ten BTLs (£1,000) – you decide.

From this position you can now create your ideal life and create an ideal pyramid to support it – have fun!

Adding in the Capital Strategies

Moving into the capital tiers of the pyramid generally happens inadvertently and I suggest that, at the beginning, you allow that to happen naturally as you go about your new property business.

So, when you go looking for your BTLs you will find some properties that need attention, and that's when you evaluate the B&F possibility. Many people do a combined B&F and BTL strategy, whereby they find a B&F property that needs attention, do it up and then drop the property into the BTL tier of their pyramid.

So they are gaining some capital value in the property immediately – which may also enable them to refinance if they want to do that – and then they are getting the regular ongoing income.

The same can happen for the larger CPs. You will just come across very run-down properties on your normal route to looking for standard income-generating properties, and then you have choices:

- It may be a clean CP, which you do up and sell.
- It may be a property that can be converted into an HMO along

the way and then dropped into the HMO tier of the pyramid as an income generator.

- Or it may be a property that gets done up and dropped into the BTL tier.

It is more sensible, and less risky, to take this 'inadvertent' approach to capital strategy properties at the beginning as a CP takes time and money and when you're not very experienced those things have a tendency to run away with you until, before you know it, you're in trouble.

I know it looks tantalising to make a big hit early on, and if you pull off a big CP deal that's great, but if you get it wrong then it may end your property business before you've even got started, dent your confidence and take all your cash.

However, once you have built up your knowledge and skills and have some income flowing such that you can feed the family, then taking on a CP is a logical step.

Fancy Pants Deals (FPD)

In the main, most people should *not* do FPDs! An FPD is, for instance, the development of twenty houses on a plot of land, or converting a factory into ten flats, or a set of farm buildings into a mini housing estate.

They tend to be big and expensive and involve expertise that most of us don't have. However, can be very profitable! So, if you do want to get a slice of that particular profit cake then I suggest you join forces with someone, or a group, and take part in an FPD joint venture.

I'm very proud of the fact that when we set up our property education company, we at Fielding Financial included the ability to facilitate that; now, all of our customers, students, trainers and mentors (me included!) have the opportunity to invest together on FPDs.

So, for instance, we've converted a property that had been empty and boarded up for two years into a set of six flats and three houses. We did that as a group and all chipped in and reaped the rewards.

And there are several benefits to doing that sort of deal as a group:

- It involves less financial exposure for each individual – in fact they invest as little or as much as they want.

- It gives every participant an opportunity to get access to the higher profit end of the pyramid.

- It's a learning opportunity for all involved, so all participants can see how the project is managed (we always employ a project manager), reported and controlled.

- It's a safer, practical route to getting knowledge, and an opportunity to complete a pyramid.

After a few of those, and possibly if you already have some experience, then doing FPDs on your own might be for you!

Advanced Strategy: Combining the Market

Now this is really for advanced investors who have a mature portfolio and are safe financially, but it's an interesting concept even for the uninitiated to think about as they start their investing.

There are naturally times when the external property market is more conducive to capital strategies and times when it's more conducive to income strategies.

I must stress that you must put your own strategy first and continue on your plan and one that will work for you, but when you have a full pyramid and the luxury of sitting there waiting to cherry-pick the next deal, consider this:

The market moves like a jelly – wibble, wobble all the time, up and down in little spurts and occasionally in bigger trends, all within its overall main upwards trend. As those wobbles occur they create different opportunities due to the behaviour of the populace.

When the property market is rising, the general public get confident in the market and tend to want to buy their own houses and, as the market rises, people who already own homes realise they have made a gain and want to trade up to something larger.

So, as the market goes up the public tend to buy and buy bigger, and it naturally becomes a capital strategy market overall.

As the market rises, it creates the opportunity for increased value and profit over and above that which we generate as part of our business. So we buy a property that has a few strands of UPWARDS in it and we know that we will make profit, but if you add in the rising market, which we don't plan for necessarily, then that profit or gain gets larger.

Conversely, there may be fewer potential tenants around (although demand is so high that this doesn't have a great impact) as they are now buying rather than renting, so our income strategies take a slight back seat.

As the market rises, experienced investors flex their strategies to focus on capital. Then, when the market dips, the opposite behaviour occurs: the public at large lose their confidence in the market and decide to wait before they buy – and while they're waiting they have to rent.

And in that case, demand for our rental properties increases and we move our income strategies to the front seat and our capital ones move to the back.

The market doesn't travel in a straight line; it wibbles and wobbles and waves, and by riding the market waves in this way, emphasising different strategies at different times, we can maximise the amount of profit, income and gain overall and we can ensure that we make our business work most effectively whether the market is going up down or sideways!

Now this is a biggie… Any fool can make money when the market is rising and when demand is incredibly high, but a professional will generally make *more* money as the market dips, and it's this ability to create profits whatever the market is doing that really distinguishes the amateur from the professional.

So, if you look at the chart below I have highlighted four different strategic periods for my investing over the last ten years and, in each case, I made very good profits of between £500k and £1m on each of the strategies indicated.

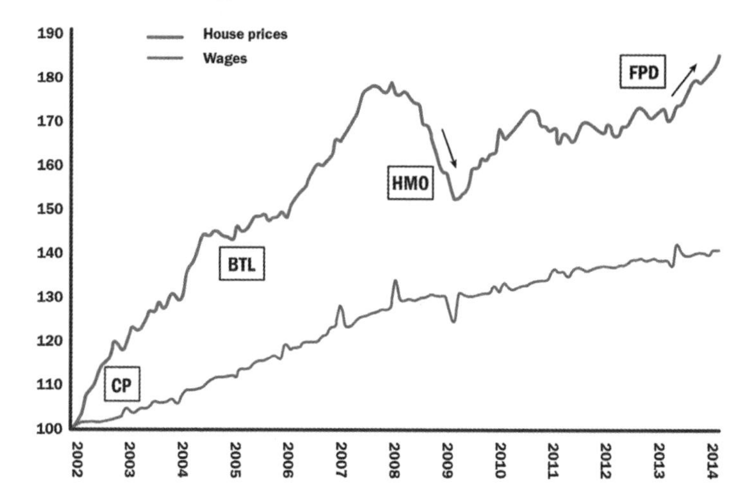

It's obviously no coincidence that the HMO strategy made the most money when the market was falling and the CP and the FPD made the most as it was rising.

Then look at the BTL, which was a combined income and capital strategy as, at the time, I was buying little cheap and cheerful properties hand over fist as the market was moving up. Financial regulation was very relaxed and I was able to buy properties on credit cards and then refinance them, bringing my money out to reinvest in new BTL as the market rose.

We can't do that in that way anymore. If we want to do that we need access to private money.

In summary, then, if you get good at property investing, treat it like a profession and get very well-educated and keep up to date with the market, regulatory changes and the wider financial world; then your profits and gains will be much greater!

The more you know and the better your experience, the greater your choices and profits will be.

New Build and Off Plan

I can't leave the strategy section without a brief paragraph or two about buying off plan and buying new builds – and it will be short because I don't like these at all! I can say with my hand on heart that I've never, ever bought a new build or bought a property off plan because for me they're too risky. And they're risky because there's loads of stuff you don't know!

I'm a cautious and safe investor and I check everything before I part with my money, and with new builds and off plans you can't do that. I can't check the rent, find a potential tenant, compare values and other information – all because the property doesn't exist yet.

Added to that, these properties are never alone – so they're in a block or on an estate with loads of other identical properties, so if I want to rent mine out I'm immediately in competition with other people trying to do exactly the same. That distorts the rentals and the return on my cash and I don't like that!

Finally, the evidence is that new build properties don't go up in value anywhere near as much as an existing property.

Just look at the table below, which compares the price rises, over ten years, of new properties compared with existing properties (labelled here as 'period' properties):

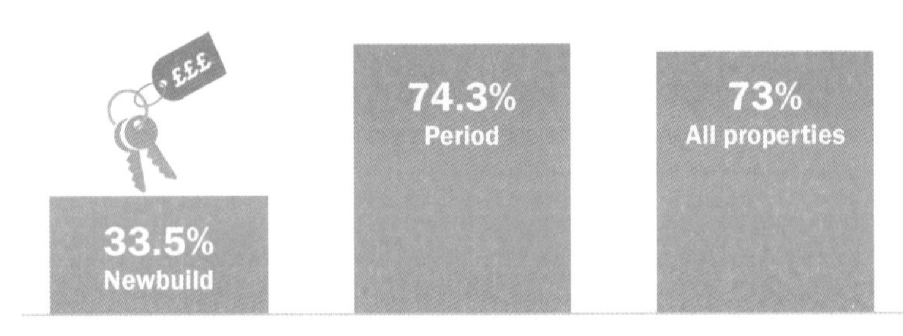

If that doesn't put you off new build then you need to look at it again!

Interesting, isn't it? And it's obvious when we think about it. With a new anything – whether it's a house or a car – a premium part of its value is in the fact that it's new; as soon as it's used the value stalls or drops, and then has to play catch-up with the market in general.

So let's illustrate the point with an example. If I bought two properties today – one a new build of £600k and one an existing property of £600k – *if* (and that's a big if, of course) values increased by the same percentages in the next ten years as they did in the last, this is what happens:

New build of £600k increasing in value by 33.5% will be worth:	£801,000
Existing property of £600k increasing in value by 74.3% will be:	£1,045,800
Total 'excess' on the existing property over the new build:	**£244,800**

Of course, as a professional investor I look at these things – what interests me is my return, my potential gain and the balance of my strategy and my portfolio – so when I evaluate a proposition like this I can do it coldly and mathematically as I have done here. And by doing that, and taking any emotion out of the decision, the decision becomes very clear. It's a no-brainer – I wouldn't turn down an opportunity of an extra £244,800 just to buy a new build property that smelled nice.

However, I do have to say that if you're looking to buy your own home and you're not interested in the long-term gain as I am, then new builds are great! They're just not for investment.

Potential Strategy: Empty Homes

Now, the basics of this strategy are: there is a high demand for property in the UK, with approximately 3.5 million private lets and over 2 million people on the social housing waiting list.

But at the other end of the spectrum we know that about 3% of all UK properties – and that's about 710,000 properties – are empty, which could be used to fill some or all of that demand if only they were inhabitable and the owner was willing.

However, it's not as easy as that.

Of the 710,000 empties: 652,000 are in private hands and, of those, 260,000 are long-term empty, which often causes a challenge with identifying the existing owner – I'll talk about that in a minute. I also suspect that many of those are in state of complete disrepair.

Then the other empties, about 58,000, are made up of state-owned, public and county council-owned properties, which we can ignore for our purposes because it's the private ones we're interested in; if we can find out who owns them, we can normally buy them, do them up and get them rented out.

And because we tend to be able to buy them relatively cheaply and sometimes get grants to do them up, and we can get them rented out easily, they are perfect properties to fit into any part of our portfolio, giving both a capital gain and a rental income.

So, if you want to have a go at this you firstly need to find properties which are near you – or near where you want to invest – and I suggest you start with the website www.emptyhomes.com.

You can download the empty homes figures by clicking on the statistics button, and on that Excel spreadsheet you will get almost five hundred local authority boroughs that have registered empty homes. So have a look around there, find your area and off you go.

But before we go charging in, why do it?

Well, there are two main reasons: firstly, they are often cheap, especially if they are estate sales where the previous owner has died, because in that instance, the new owner – the inheritor – doesn't really care about the price because it's all bonus money for them, so they don't have the emotional attachment that the original owner may have had.

In addition to that, you do find that local councils often have grants available for empty home refurbishment because they – the councils – are targeted with reducing the number of empty homes in their patch as part of their own central government funding.

So, for the last decade or so this has been a big issue for councils and they now all have to have an empty homes officer responsible for reducing the number of empties – and we'll get back to that empty homes officer later.

And secondly, we do it because the supply of housing is more or less static nowadays so we need more stock!

Right, now to the nitty-gritty – how to find them.

Start with the empty homes list we talked about earlier and see how many empties are in your area, and if there aren't many look further afield.

Then go to the local council website for the area you're interested in and click around for the empty homes section. Now, using one of my local councils as an example here, go and have a look at www.arun.gov.uk and click on the housing link. Then click on the empty homes button in the private housing section and you will get through to the empty homes page, where you will see before and after photos and all the relevant stats – including a very specific 'by borough' count of where the empties are. And if you are checking on that website you will see that there are 190 empties in Bognor Regis and another 104 in Littlehampton, where I have many properties myself.

Some local councils also do an alert service where you can register and be contacted every time the empty homes officer gets a new property on their patch, so the third place to look is the empty homes officer.

Now, every council has to have one of these but some take it more seriously than others. In some cases there are whole departments looking after empty homes while in other cases the person allocated to the task drives the mobile library on a Tuesday and does empty homes on Fridays. So it's a part-time thing for them.

We can also find these empties by just walking the streets and keeping our eyes open – and remember there might be an empty flat upstairs; it doesn't have to be the whole house. Of course, any estate agent, letting agent or sourcing agent may also know of them.

And finally, there are often many empties in auctions, and that's because for those properties that are estate sales where the owner has died, the property is being sold by an executor and they just want the deal sorted as quickly as possible. We know that with auctions the deal is usually done within twenty-eight days of the auction, so executors like that route.

There are many different places to look in to find these properties and, in many cases, the person arranging the sale will know who previously owned it and can then just arrange the sale and purchase for you; but if you just find one by walking the streets, how do you find the owner then?

Well these are my top seven ways of finding the owner:

First, see if you can find the name of the owner by looking on the local electoral roll, which you will find sometimes in libraries and always in the area's election registration office – usually the local council office. You need to go at certain times, so check your local council for opening times and availability of the register.

If that doesn't work, try the Land Registry – and as long as you have the full postal address of the property you can go online to www.landregistry.gov.uk and, for £3, you can get a copy of the property title which will give you the owner's name and many other details besides, which will come in useful when you go through the purchase.

Now, not all land is registered and if the property has been empty for a very long time there is a chance it hasn't been as compulsory registration only came in in 1990. So, any property that has been bought or sold since then will be registered, but before then it may not be and you will have to try other ways and means to find the owner's name.

Whether you have the name or not, you now write a letter to the property, addressed to the owner's name if you know it. Just address it to 'the owner' if you don't.

In the letter, you say you are interested in purchasing the property and can they get in touch with you. Now, there's a chance that the letter will be redirected either to the owner, if they have moved elsewhere, or to an executor, a local firm of solicitors or someone else who might be able to help.

If that fails you, now turn into Miss Marple or Hercule Poirot and go to the house – and then knock on neighbours' doors and say that you are thinking of moving into the area and wonder if they know who lived next door or up the road in the empty house, or if they know if the person had any relatives nearby, or if there's anyone local who might know.

Also try the same conversation with any local newsagent, corner store, church, post office, postman or lady, milkman or, frankly, any passer-by. Dog walkers tend to know quite a lot of people in an area, so if you have your own pooch, take it with you as it could be a useful prop for you there.

Then you follow all the leads accordingly.

And if all else fails you still have two more options:

Firstly, there's our friendly local empty homes officer at the council – and it *is* their responsibility to find out who owns these properties. And if that also fails, one last thing to try is to advertise!

So, put postcards in the local shop window, advertise in the local newspaper and, where possible, create a little flyer that contains the property details and your contact details. Post that through the letterboxes of the surrounding streets, and while you're at it, chat to all the people you see about the house in question!

Now, sooner or later all that will pay off and you will be inundated with empty properties that may have grants available to help you to pay for some – or all – of the refurbishment. Then you have a continual supply of cheap properties to pop into any part of your property portfolio.

CHAPTER 7

The Tool Box

What I want to include in this section is all of those other topics that we need in the toolbox before we embark on investing as our professional career, and there are many so I've covered a selection of topics in overview only. In all cases, you need to look at the subject in more detail before you leap off that cliff.

TAX

Disclaimer! Please be aware that nothing in this section is advice for you personally. I don't know your circumstances and, in most cases, any taxation question is answered differently for each person depending on their personal situation and other financial circumstances.

However, what we can cover in this section is some broad information that might be useful and which you could use to ask a more informed question of your tax advisor.

There are five taxes that could possibly impact you in your professional property investing career, and they are:

- Stamp duty.
- Income tax.
- Capital gains tax.
- Corporation tax.

And, if you still own them all when you die:

- Inheritance tax.

Three are easy to deal with:

Stamp Duty

You will pay stamp duty on the purchase of any asset, and property is no different. It is calculated as a percentage of the purchase price after deducting the first £125,000. There are different rates payable (currently between 0–12% in the tax year 2015–2016) and certain exceptions to the standard rules. Therefore with this one please just look up stamp duty on the government website and get the current information: www.gov.uk/stamp-duty-land-tax-rates.

In addition there is now an extra 3% stamp duty on the purchase of second and subsequent properties. Please see the 2016 Postscript.

Also, one quick warning relating to connected transactions. If you want to buy more than one property at the same time from the same vendor then please seek advice from your solicitor or tax advisor *before* you buy as there are separate rules that apply to connected transactions and purchases.

Corporation Tax

Corporation tax will only be payable on income and gains made on properties purchased through a company. For the moment we will only consider properties bought as individuals.

There is no legal requirement to set up a company and there can be some disadvantages to it. If you want to buy with two or more other people then that can legally be done as a partnership or group of individuals.

Please seek advice!

Inheritance Tax

Your estate will pay inheritance tax if you die with assets above the inheritance tax threshold, which is, at the time of writing, £325,000.

If you think this may affect you or your estate then please seek professional advice.

Income Tax

For most new investors this is the one tax that impacts them straight away, as tax is due on any profits from the property business almost immediately.

There are separate pages of the annual tax return specifically for rental properties and you can click on those, if you do your tax return online, or ask your HMRC office or your tax advisor for copies if you need to receive them in paper format.

Unless you know your circumstances are different from most people's, tax is payable on the net income receivable from your properties in each tax year – that being the 6th April in one year to 5th April the following year. Taxation is due to be reported to HMRC – if you report online – by the 31st January following the end of the tax year.

So, if the tax year is 6th April 2015–5th April 2016, the return needs to be submitted by the 31st January 2017.

So What Do We Need to Report?

Rents

Firstly the rents: report the total rents receivable from all the properties added together for that tax year. You do not need to report rents on individual properties but keep the detailed figures just in case you need them later.

Less Allowable Expenses

Allowable expenses are:

- Rates, insurance, service charges, ground rents.
- Repairs and maintenance.
- Finance charges – incurred in obtaining the loan.
- Finance charges – the interest on borrowings (see postscript).
- Legal and professional fees.
- Service costs such as cleaning and gardening.
- Advertising.
- Letting agents' fees, including the VAT if they charge you that.
- A portion of home bills if you work from home (but not the cost of an entire room as that may impact your Principle Private Residence Relief – see the capital gains tax section below).
- Cost of ongoing training/books/courses.
- Portion of car costs or 45p per mile (for the first ten thousand miles, and then it drops down to 25p per mile).
- Motorbike costs – 24p per mile.
- Push bike use – 20p per mile.

Plus

There are quite a lot of allowable deductions and, once you take them off the rents you receive, you then pay tax on what's left over; consequently, the amount of tax payable tends to be small.

Please seek professional advice.

Capital Gains Tax (CGT)

CGT is effectively an optional tax as you only need to pay it when you sell a property; so if you don't want to pay CGT then don't sell anything!

Of course that may be unrealistic, so what is payable and how is it calculated?

Well, CGT is payable on the net of the sales proceeds less:

- Purchase cost (which includes any stamp duty).
- Any capital cost for enhancements to the property.
- Sales or realisation costs.

Then, once you have calculated what's left, you are allowed to deduct your annual CGT allowance (currently £11,100 for the 2015–2016 tax year), and then you pay CGT on what's left after that.

NB: you do not pay CGT when you sell your own home as you get Principle Private Residence relief for that.

LEGAL AND SAFETY

OK, let's get the warning over with!

Nothing in this section is legal advice or intended to be such. This is purely a swift guide to what seems, to me, to be important. Please seek legal advice where needed.

Let's start with some basic definitions:

Definition One – What's a Freehold?

- A freeholder, or one who is in freehold, originally was not a vassal.

- In medieval times, people were tied to – or were vassals of – the lord of the manor or king, and a freehold meant you were free of that feudal system because you had your own land and property.

- For an estate to be a freehold it must possess two qualities:

  - *Immobility* (so you can't move it about).

  - *Ownership* of it must be of an indeterminate duration. If the time of ownership can be fixed and determined, then it's not freehold.

- When you buy something freehold you get to own the land and all immovable structures attached to such land.

- Immovable structures include land and all that naturally goes with it, such as buildings and trees, but not such things as vehicles or livestock (which move).

- You also own the underground resources and the air above it (up to a level not yet legally determined, but clearly aircraft and satellites, etc. aren't in *your* space).

Definition Two – What's a Flying Freehold?

If we understand that a normal freehold covers all the space between the earth and the sky, we can see and understand that no two freeholds can overlap. If they do, then there's a flying freehold somewhere where the overlap occurs.

Definition Three – When is a Freehold not 'Free'?

Property may not necessarily be free of encumbrances, so there may be:

- Rights of way over your land.
- Covenants, which may restrict what you can do without payment.

So, for instance, there may be a religious or specific right of access. Please check!

Definition Four – What's a Leasehold?

A leasehold is the internal 'bits' of a freehold, which are:

- Issued/sold separately for a set period of anything up to 999 years.
- Saleable independently of the freehold.
- Expirable, at which time the lease reverts to the freeholder.

The freehold–leasehold relationship is a bit like Russian dolls: the external doll is the freehold and all the other dolls inside are leaseholds.

Does It Matter Which I Have?

Well, with freeholds there are no specific issues that result of the ownership, but with leaseholds there are two main problems: financing and maintenance.

Financing Leasehold Purchases

- Most fund providers will only lend on leaseholds if there's seventy-five to eighty years left in the lease (it equates to about the lives of two mortgages).
- But as a leaseholder, you can apply for a lease extension when there's eighty years or fewer left on the lease.
- The longer left on the lease, the cheaper it is to extend – if there's only a little time then the freeholder is entitled to a lot! This is known as the 'marriage value'.

But...

The 1993 Leasehold Reform Act says you have the right to extend (generally for 125 years) if:

- You are over twenty-one.
- You have owned the leasehold for at least two years.
- You know the ground rent, the lease details and the value of the property at the time, which are needed to calculate the lease extension cost.

www.lease-advice.org.uk will give you an approximate cost to lease extensions.

The Leasehold Valuation Tribunal will negotiate between the leaseholder and the freeholder if necessary.

You can also *buy* the freehold (if the freeholder agrees) and, more importantly, the freeholder *cannot sell* the freehold without offering it to the existing leaseholder/s first under the Landlord and Tenant Act 1987.

Maintenance and the Right to Manage (RTM)

If you have difficulties with the freeholder over maintenance of the property you do have the right, under the Commonhold and Leasehold Reform Act 2002, to manage the property yourself – or to appoint a new management company – irrespective of reason, as long as you give the correct notice and:

- More than two-thirds of the flats are let to 'qualifying tenants'[3].
- Any commercial part of the block is not greater than 25%.

There is no requirement for any past or present residence in the flats, nor any limit on the number of flats that can be owned by one person. The RTM does not apply where the premises fall within the Resident Landlord Exemption. To fulfil this exemption would require the following:

- The premises must be other than a purpose-built block.
- They must be comprised of not more than four flats.
- For the last twelve months, 25% of the flats must have been occupied by the freeholder, or an adult member of their family, as their only or principal home.

The Right to Manage may only be exercised by an RTM company, and the members of the RTM company must be comprised of a sufficient

3 A 'qualifying tenant' is a leaseholder whose lease was originally granted for a term of more than twenty-one years.

number of qualifying tenants (equal to at least half the total number of flats in the building).

Tenants and the Law

A landlord's responsibility to tenants starts even before that tenant is identified because advertising for tenants has to comply with legislation in regard of race, gender, ethnicity and nationality. In addition, you cannot advertise for tenants based on religion, nor can you offer different terms and conditions for different groups of people. But you *can* advertise for a non-smoker with GSOH! Once the tenant is identified then there are four areas to cover:

- References.
- The tenancy agreement.
- The deposit.
- Checking them in and inventory.

References

To be certain then, obtain references and supporting evidence to cover:

- Employment – ask them to show you payslips as well as the reference itself.
- Tenancy – get a letter from a previous landlord.
- Financial stability – get a credit check.
- Your gut feel!

There are tenant referencing agencies that will do all of this for you, such as:

- **www.tenantreferencecheck.co.uk**

- **www.experian.co.uk/background-checking/tenant-check.html**

- **www.rentchecks.com**

- **www.landlords.org.uk**

Also, consider getting a guarantor if:

- The tenant has no previous letting experience.

- The tenant reference isn't quite right.

Make sure you get a guarantor who is a homeowner and on the electoral roll, and for student houses get each parent for each student – and get references in the same way for guarantors as you do for tenants.

Ongoing, get on the guarantor's case quickly if there's a problem.

Tenancy Agreements

Obviously, the main tenancy agreement in the UK is the Assured Shorthold Tenancy agreement, which:

- Is the most common.

- Is regulated by Code in the Housing Act 1988 (and updated).

- Allows a landlord to charge a market rent.

- Allows a landlord to recover a property relatively easily, under Section 21.
- Lasts, usually, for at least six months.
- Allows a landlord to create a specific and comprehensive agreement to suit the property, as long as they cover the minimum requirements – see below.

Basics

The tenant must be an individual – not a company – and the property must be the main home of the occupant. Also, the property has to be let as separate accommodation (i.e. not sharing), and the landlord must normally provide two months' notice when asking the tenants to leave. The minimum to include in an agreement is:

- Landlord's name.
- Tenant's name.
- The property address.
- The date the AST will start and end – so, duration.
- The amount of rent and when and how payable.
- Details of who pays anything else: council tax, utilities, etc.
- What the landlord is going to do, e.g. maintenance.
- What the tenant is expected to do.

Tenant responsibilities are:

- To pay the agreed rent in full and on time.

- To make sure no damage is caused to the property or its contents, whether by the tenant, members of the household or visitors.

- To consult the landlord about making any alterations to the property and requesting written permission.

- To report any damage or need for repairs to the landlord.

- To not cause disturbance, or annoyance to neighbours.

- To provide the landlord with access to the property for the purpose of inspection, or to carry out repairs, as long as sufficient notice has been provided.

- To obtain written permission from the landlord if they want to sublet or take in a lodger.

- To give the agreed amount of notice to the landlord if the tenant wishes to terminate the agreement and leave the property.

- To not leave the property unoccupied for longer than fourteen days without informing the landlord or managing agent.

Tenant rights are:

- To know the full terms of the tenancy agreement.

- To know the name and address of the landlord.

- To reside in a property that is in adequate condition for rental purposes, free from defects.

- To receive reasonably prompt repairs and maintenance.

- To live in safe accommodation, with all equipment, gas and electrical systems meeting the required safety standards.

- To have a Gas Safe registered Gas Safety Inspection Certificate produced annually and at the start of each tenancy.

- To have peaceable and quiet enjoyment of the property, free from demands for access without prior notification, or interference with utilities or other supplies to the property.

- To have a rent book if the rent is payable weekly.

- A reasonable statutory period of notice if the landlord wants the agreement to end.

- To have the security deposit returned within a reasonable period of time (within thirty days), subject to the necessary checks on the property and up-to-date rental payments.

Landlord responsibilities are:

- To allow tenants to reside in the property without disturbance.

- To make reasonably prompt repairs and undertake maintenance to the property if required.

- To maintain the structure and exterior of the property; hot water installations and water supply; electrical wiring; basins, baths, sinks and toilets, etc.

- To ensure the building complies with building regulations.

- To ensure that all gas appliances are safely maintained by Gas Safe registered engineers.

- To make sure all electrical equipment is safe to use.

- To provide furniture (if the property is furnished) that meets the necessary fire-resistant regulations.

- To provide and maintain fire alarms, fire extinguishers, fire blankets, fire escapes and smoke or heat alarms.

In addition, the landlord must have the right to let the property out in the first place – so check:

- With mortgaged properties: obtain permission from the mortgage company if it is not a specialist buy-to-let mortgage. A Consent to Let is usually required.

- Leasehold: check the lease and obtain permission from the freeholder if necessary.

- Check if planning permission is needed (this mostly relates to HMOs).

- Check whether a licence from the local authority is needed (this mostly relates to HMOs).

Landlord rights are:

- To repossess the property if the rent remains unpaid for fourteen days or more, where the tenant breaches the terms of the tenancy or becomes bankrupt or enters into an arrangement with creditors.

- To dispose of any property left at the premises unclaimed within a specified period of time.

- To enter the property, after providing the tenant with reasonable notice of doing so (usually twenty-four hours).

- To seek possession of the property if the tenant has damaged it.

- To collect overdue rent payments from the tenant.

NB: if the tenancy contains a break clause, either the landlord or the tenant can exercise this after the first six months of the tenancy.

Inventory and Checking In

- Do an inventory – even if it's just a description of empty rooms with nothing in – and take photos!

- Get the tenant to sign the inventory – on every page – as you take them round and check them in.

- Show the tenant the meter readings and get them to check and sign those on the agreement.

- Make sure that the tenant signs every page of the agreement.

Deposits

Rules apply to *all* deposits received after 6th April 2007. Watch if you buy a tenanted property where the tenancy started before then.

Tenants' deposits have to be safeguarded in one of four schemes (check web for current providers). And the deposit has to be remitted within thirty days of *receipt* – not the tenancy start date.

At the end of the tenancy – if all parties agree – then the deposit must be returned within ten days.

Deposit Disputes

Each scheme has a free service which landlords and tenants can use to sort out disagreements about deposits, instead of going to court. This is called an alternative dispute resolution (ADR) service.

The ADR service will decide how much of the deposit you should get back. The tenancy deposit scheme will then pay you the money.

Can a Landlord Increase the Rent?

A landlord *can't* do this unless:

- It's in the tenancy agreement.

- When the agreement ends the landlord issues a new agreement detailing the new rent.

- The landlord issues a Schedule 8 notice, which can be clunky, time-consuming and cumbersome; so, ideally insist on a new agreement every six months.

Evicting a Tenant

There are two main routes private landlords can take to regain possession of their property under the Housing Act 1988:

- Section 21 given at *any* time gives a landlord an automatic right of possession without having to give any grounds once the fixed term has expired.

- Section 8 allows a landlord to seek possession using grounds 2, 8, 10 to 15 or 17 listed in Schedule 2 to the Act. These include rent arrears and antisocial behaviour.

The Schedule 2 main causes are:

- Rent arrears.
- Dilapidation of the property.
- Breach of terms of the AST.
- Nuisance to neighbours.
- Provision of false information.

Under these circumstances, the landlord can apply for a court order and, if successful, the court will normally evict in fourteen days, but can take up to six weeks.

Energy Performance Certificate

A landlord also has to provide an Energy Performance Certificate (EPC). These were designed to give tenants and buyers more information about the energy efficiency of a building. The subtext is to create a market for energy efficiency in buildings.

The EPC is intended to give an idea of the cost of heating and lighting per annum and it is a legal requirement to have one for each building being sold or rented, and to make an EPC available at the earliest opportunity. The EPC must include an asset graph with written particulars.

A Word on Insurances

You have to insure the buildings, but other insurances, such as contents, are optional and depend on the agreement with the tenant.

However, please make sure your policy includes Property Owners Public Liability up to something like £5 million of cover. This will allow you to sleep at night and will cover you against death, injury or damage to individuals on or near your property, for example tenants, visitors and guests, meter readers and postmen, etc.

Local authorities and universities will normally specify a minimum amount of cover needed when you house housing benefit tenants or students. Please check that you have sufficient and suitable insurance cover with your insurance broker.

VIEWING TIPS

When we first get started in our investing most of us have little or no idea how to view a property – and at that stage have only experienced the (generally quite embarrassing) look round a property that we want to buy for our own home.

Those viewings are normally complete with the existing owner helpfully pointing out every feature, fireplace and plughole as you go round.

Like most things in property viewing, the domestic residential option bears very little similarity to the viewing prior to an investment purchase and, once again, I find myself saying that this is a skill you need to acquire before you can be turned from the accidental and amateur investor into the true professional.

I will cover the specifics of internal viewing in a later session but what I want to address here are the fourteen points to cover when planning your viewings – before you even get to the property – together with a few after-viewing tips.

So where do we start?

1 When you are planning a buying trip to a new town, buy a street map of the area in advance and spend some time familiarising yourself with the main streets. You can order street maps for towns outside your own area at most large newsagents or online.

   Get used to getting the street maps of towns and develop your own colour coding system indicating where to buy and where to avoid. Also, highlight the main areas of investment, where the bulk of the HMOs might be and where the fancy pants houses are and so on. Keep these coded maps in your office so that you have them for future reference.

2 Plan your potential viewings and if you are planning several viewings in a town, particularly one that is new to you, be realistic about the number that you can accommodate in an hour, remembering to factor in travel time, getting lost time

and losing the street on the map time.

It's better to plan to accommodate a few viewings per hour, and be able to spend a considered amount of time at each property, than it is to have to rush from one to another, risking upsetting the viewing representative or missing an important factor at a property.

Obviously it makes sense – if you can – to 'block view' a few streets at a time so you can see a lot of properties in a very close location quickly.

3 Be organised and have a list! Have all your property viewings listed on a single worksheet or use a day-per-page diary with hourly time dividers.

As a minimum, record the street address; property style and selling price; postcode; agent's company name and contact number; viewing representative name, if known, and street map grid reference. By having the agent's contact details conveniently to hand, if you are lost or running late, you can easily call the agent to explain your circumstances.

4 Make a viewing summary sheet for each property and record basic details such as property type and condition; location; neighbourhood and amenities; asking price and the contact details of other agents with similar properties in the area. Even if you do not purchase the property, attach the viewing summary sheet to the sales particulars; then file them when you get home in a viewings archive – you will be surprised at how valuable this record will be over time for looking back at the market when you revisit that area later, as your portfolio develops.

5 If you are planning a viewing day, be practical about what you need for the types of property you will be viewing. Be prepared for properties being more run-down than the sales blurb suggests, so dress accordingly and don't be surprised by what you might find in the front garden. You may encounter the

traditional garden features such as cars in various states of disrepair, broken prams and bedsteads. Or more surprising features such as trip hazards left by begrudging occupants, needles left by unwelcome guests or mess left by the local feral cats.

Practical shoes, a brolly, torch, damp meter, clipboard and digital camera are the staple accessories of the earnest property investor.

6 If you are travelling away from home to spend a day or two viewing be sure that you book your viewings in advance. Many estate agents have full viewing books and if you turn up unannounced to look at some properties you see in the window, they may not be able to provide you with a viewing space in the diary for a day or two. Also, be aware that some agents only conduct viewings on certain days of the week, and that you will need to be in the town *on that day* and have an appointment booked if you want to view at all. In such a situation it is very likely that a heartfelt plea to view on another day will fall on deaf ears.

7 Think about whether you need to stay locally and book some accommodation – maybe at a centrally located hotel or a guest house with a practical lounge – which can also be useful if you're arranging out-of-hours meetings with letting or sourcing agents.

The Tourist Information office in the town will know all of the major accommodation providers in the area and they can be found through Directory Enquiries.

If you have not done much pre-trip preparation in advance, the Tourist Information office is also a valuable resource as a first stop for research in a new town. Many will provide a list of letting agents and estate agents and a free map, which they can mark up for you, so that you can plan your trips around the agents in the most time-efficient manner, moving from district to district around the area.

8 In conjunction with a copy of the local paper, or a listing of estate agents and letting agents, mark the locations of their offices on the street map you ordered in advance before you leave home – it will save time in the field and means that you can travel straight to agents on your arrival without having to stop to ask for directions.

9 Before you leave home, order a copy of the main local newspaper servicing the area that you are visiting so that you can familiarise yourself with prices and agents.

When you place an order over the phone with the sales desk of the local paper, be sure to check which day the property section is published. You can receive the local paper either by post, or via delivery through your local newsagent – check with them for details.

10 However confident you are in your powers of memory, after a full day of viewing similar properties, when you come to review them, after returning to your hotel room or home, you may be surprised how they all merge into one. Distinguishing the one with the serious subsidence from the one that needs new gutters becomes a real challenge. With your digital camera, take pictures of problem items, the outside of the house *and* the neighbourhood to jog your memory.

More sophisticated cameras have a voice memo facility and you can record the property address along with your pictures. If your camera has a short movie clip facility, consider recording a steady pan shot up and down the street, on either side of the front door, to act as a record of the environs. If you decide to buy the house, this clip will act as a valuable historical record of how the area changes over the years of your ownership.

11 Create a viewing checklist summary sheet to keep on your clipboard, where you record key property details – address, agent, asking price, defects, area appraisal and number of and description of rooms and their conditions.

The form needs to be sufficiently detailed to act as an aide-memoire when you do your property reviews back at base, but not so detailed that you spend most of your time in the property slavishly completing the form and not enough time considering the property overall. No more than one or two sides of A4 is sufficient. Even for the properties that you pass over, staple the summary sheet to the sales particulars and file them in your viewings history box file. You may get offered the property a year or two later and the defect that you originally spotted may be covered or patched over. Your diligence in reviewing your original appraisal will pay off, firstly by helping you to appear clued up when you question the vendor about the matter in the first place and secondly by helping you to ensure that the defect has been suitably rectified.

Also consider adding to your checklist an area where you can jot down personal details about the current owner and how they use the house. It may come in handy later, if you have to contact the owner. If you know, for instance, that they have dogs and a piano it gives you a topic of conversation that you can use to establish rapport with them. This is particularly useful if you are at a distance and cannot get to see them face to face.

12 Be respectful and bear in mind the needs of the other parties in the viewing. Your estate agent or keyholder will typically have a busy viewing schedule to accommodate and will not be able to wait forever if you are running late. Most viewing agents will wait ten minutes for you to arrive to allow for traffic and delays but after that they will move on to their next appointment. Even if you call ahead to notify them of your late running, don't be surprised if they say that they cannot wait and request that

you rebook. If the vendor is doing the viewing and it is their own home you may have more flexibility if you are running late; however if the vendor is not living in the property and is also travelling to the premises to meet you there, the same consideration applies as if a viewing agent were doing the viewing.

13 When you get back to base, prepare three piles of viewing sheets – they are your 'Yes', 'No' and 'Maybe' piles.

Focus your immediate attention on your 'Yes' and then your 'Maybe' piles. Your 'Yes' pile should contain those properties that you have identified as clearly offering the potential for a deal. You may like to create a set of criteria that properties in the 'Yes' pile have to pass. For example:

- There is clear evidence for a discounted or well-structured purchase.
- There is evidence of scope for improvement that will add measurable value to the property.
- The property is in an area of firm demand.
- You expect that the property will be of demand when the time for sale comes.
- Any refurbishments that are required are within the scope of your present team and budget.
- Comparables from at least three estate agents and letting agents stack up.

Your 'Maybe' pile could contain properties that only pass, say, four of the six tests, or have another feature that requires further investigation.

For those properties in your 'Yes' pile, carefully run the

numbers with a conservative perspective on the market, your transaction costs, refurbishment, if required, and rental figures. Satisfy yourself that you can stand the property being refurbished or empty for longer than expected.

When you're ready, prepare your offer and present it to the agent, or the vendor, having carefully checked all the numbers – at least twice! Also factor in seasonal aspects of the market – if your property is going on the market in the traditionally slower period of November to February, consider that you may have to wait longer for a taker, or that your price may need to be lower than in the more buoyant periods of the year.

Once your offer is accepted, don't be afraid of requesting a second (or maybe even a third) viewing. It is absolutely essential that you are fully acquainted with your prospective purchase, its defects, the immediate neighbours and the neighbourhood. Redo your sums in the light of any builders' quotes that you may have received since the first viewing, and use them as a negotiating tactic if mandatory work is required on areas such as damp, roofing or remedial wood treatments.

14 And finally, here's one tip for viewing an auction property: with properties for sale through auction, the viewing time is usually specified so you are allowed to look at the property, for instance, on Tuesday between 12 and 2pm.

One student of ours duly trotted along at the appointed time to find that the property was in good condition. There were a nice couple in the property – the tenants – and the property was clean and relatively well-maintained. Overall it looked promising, but the client had that niggle that made him feel that it wasn't quite right somehow. So, on the way to the auction where he intended to bid for the property, he took the trouble to drive past the property again.

This time he saw the property in its true state – with rubbish in the front plus an old car being dismantled on the lawn. He knocked on the door to discover that it was inhabited not by a middle-aged couple but by a large number of unconnected people.

What appeared to be relatively clean was now in total disarray and looked dirty and unkempt.

Remember, if something doesn't feel quite right keep asking, viewing and checking until you feel better – or walk away from the deal.

And that's it: fourteen tips to plan viewings – and as usual the guidance is to be efficient and professional, and then you'll make the best use of your time and efforts.

PRESENTING A PROFITABLE PROPERTY

A fundamental part of any property investor's skill is being able to provide the property that people want – and of course to avoid the ones that people don't! So I always read those lists of 'property turn-offs' to make sure that I'm still on track with my product.

In fact, this could even result in an entire strategy because so many people get the fundamentals wrong – so buy a property cheap that's been presented badly and then correct it and sell it on; that would work.

According to my research the top twenty turn-offs that put people off when looking at either buying or renting a property are:

Top Twenty Property Turn-Offs

Rank	Top Twenty Property Turn-Offs	%
1	Damp patches, stained walls and ceilings	70
2	Property in poor state of repair (e.g. rotten windows)	63
3	No garden	57
4	Bad smells, including odours from pets, cigarette smoke, damp and food	56
5	No parking	56
6	Poor natural light; dark rooms	54
7	Unfinished building work	54
8	Small rooms	51
9	Small kitchen	44
10	Bad DIY	43
11	Dirty house	37
12	Stone cladding, render or pebbledash on outside walls	31
13	Outdated bathroom	25
14	Outdated kitchen	25
15	Artex or textured ceilings	18
16	Plastic windows	18
17	Overgrown garden	16
18	General untidiness	16
19	Cluttered rooms	15
20	Dated or over-the-top décor	14

Now, when we look at that list we can divide the potential problems into two groups: those things you can do nothing about, like the lack of a garden, and those things that you can do plenty about – like the smells and the clutter.

I'm now going to give you the top seven tips for presenting a property to its best advantage.

So **Tip Number One** has to be to give the property a B&F, and I would cover in that the following:

Repair when you can. For example, damp patches will just keep coming back if you don't resolve the underlying problem, so don't just paint it with fancy water-protective paint – get to the root of the problem, solve it and then paint it once.

Likewise with any superficial damage like broken windows or doors, broken cupboards or hinges – just get a decent general odd-job person who will go round the property with a toolbox and some elbow grease and fix all those fiddly things.

The problem you have if you don't fix those things is that they become an annoyance and a niggle that the potential purchaser will focus on – if you can give them a sensible property with the basics sorted, they can then view the property without that niggle.

People may think, 'Well, it's only a broken cupboard door and it'll only cost £20 to fix it so I won't bother – I'll just knock £20 off the sales price.' Well, if it's only £20 then *fix it* because it'll cost you a lot more if you lose the buyer.

It can sometimes be difficult to see all those niggles if you've had a property for a long time because you get used to the fact that you can only shut the cupboard door if you swing it from left to right and push at the top at the same time – that action may have become second nature and subconscious to you because you've done it so many times; but I can assure you that a person looking at it for the first time *will* see a problem.

If you know a property *too* well then you need to get someone else to look at it for you and list the niggle nightmares and then you just get them fixed. This is a service we can do for each other as it doesn't need a professional's eye, it just needs common sense – do this as a service swap for another investor in our property family.

Number One then is to repair the niggles, and if you can't repair them totally then at least neaten the problem.

Tip Number Two has to be about the clutter! There is some kind of filtering ability in our own brains that means we don't notice our own clutter – but other people do! So I have developed the one-third rule for clutter and that works very simply.

All you have to do is remove one-third of everything! So in a house, remove one-third of the furniture if you can. From every wardrobe take out one-third of all the clothes, hats, shoes and sundry clutter and put those in suitcases in the loft. Now, what you have in your wardrobe is of no relevance to any potential property purchaser at all as we assume you are taking your clothes with you – but if a potential purchaser does look in your wardrobe on a viewing that will help create a good impression.

Likewise, remove one-third of all ornaments, pictures, books and tit-and-tat that you have lying around your home and store it all in boxes, preferably at an off-site storage facility.

I have even seen properties where the owner has removed one-third of kitchen cabinets and other fitted furniture including bookshelves and so on. My only slight hesitation about this is that I like fixed-type storage, so please be careful not to sacrifice one bonus in your property for another in this case.

Tip Number Three is to look at your property from the outside in. Apparently, a potential purchaser makes their buying decision from the pavement outside so it makes sense to make the outside look right, and that means painting the front door a bright, solid colour (and apparently a dark blue or dark red works best) and also clearing the area around the front door so it looks clear, clean and fresh. Then *please* take all the junk mail and kids' wellies from behind the front door before you show people round.

Tip Number Four is to depersonalise, so take out the personal and emotional stuff – like wedding photos and the baby's handprint cast.

Tip Number Five is to take out anything that might threaten a potential viewer – and this includes your gun collection, the sabre over the fireplace and your Rottweiler dog. And I include in this category anything that most people find bizarre, like your collection of whips – now that probably fails on account of being both personal *and* threatening!

Tip Number Six is to go visiting show homes on new housing developments because the designer who prepared the show home will have known every presentation trick in the book, from three-quarter-sized furniture to glass-topped tables which show the floor through and consequently give the illusion of space. You will also find in there curtains that could never close, mirrors opposite every natural light source and furniture with drawers so thin that you couldn't even put your socks away.

I don't think anyone ever intended anybody to live in properties furnished and equipped like that – clearly in a lot of cases it's just impossible – but the concept of presenting a property to its maximum advantage, like a product in a shop window, is an interesting one and we can learn a lot from looking at examples and adapting the ideas to our property.

And **Tip Number Seven** is this: *clean* the property – and then clean it again. Remove stains, smells, dirt, grime, grease and rubbish. Clean the floors, carpets, ceilings, woodwork, furniture, fixtures, fittings, windows, doors, knobs, knockers and knick-knacks.

Just clean. And if I could do only one thing to prepare a property it would be this – and it would actually eliminate at least four of the top twenty put-offs that we started with in this section.

Most of the top twenty things that put people off renting or buying your property can be *easily* and *cheaply* solved. Many people think that they may as well just leave it as is and then sell the house to a highest bidder but, sadly, if you don't do anything then there may never be any bidders! A bit of industry and input will go a long way and you will get a massive return on your money and effort.

It is fair to say though that this depends on the market itself, and if we are in a massively high-demand phase or area then nothing much matters and the property will sell. However, for the average rent or buy property then these small things go a long way to making sure your property investing business is efficient and effective.

So go and get your cleaning cloth now and make yourself some money!

THE CLOCK IS TICKING

A Selection of TIME and Diary-Based Tips for Property Investors

Now I'm going to let you into a secret – the stuff I have to do daily is a lot easier than the stuff I have to do annually.

That's it – what a tip that is – and we can all accept that if we absorb something into our daily routine it becomes, like cleaning your teeth, a mindless and innate thing to do.

And actually, anything repeated with regularity does eventually become almost second nature so it's worthwhile getting some time-based and diary-based routines absorbed into your property investing.

You may think that almost everything you do in your investing career is a reactive thing – and that's certainly true when you first get started because you don't know what's going to happen and when – but as your portfolio matures, more and more of your activity becomes a proactive thing and under your control.

Clearly, the sooner you get to that stage the better.

So I have developed routines that I do daily, quarterly and annually and I'll share some of those now – you just choose which ones you think will help you organise your property investing activities into a more controlled and predictable way of life, because that's when you get control of your time and create meaningful life choices.

Daily

- Every day make a phone call to somebody who can help you move forward – an agent, a fellow investor, the helpdesk – anybody. Just keep on keeping on.

  This helps you to stay focused, motivated and energised. Just by making the call you are taking action and you will increase your motivation (and theirs!) as a consequence. Call somebody to chat through your deals – they may be able to help you to clarify your thoughts.

- Walk, talk and behave like the investor you want to be. If you believe that successful investors get up early, wear smart clothes and drink cappuccino before nine, then do that. Whatever you think successful investors look like, sound like and behave like, adopt those characteristics until you convince yourself you *are* that successful investor.

- Every day make a connection, look at a website, read a relevant publication and discover something new about your field. None of us ever knows everything, and if we don't keep developing we stagnate.

Remember, even if you are on the right road, you will still get run over if you just sit there!

Quarterly

- Make sure you up the stakes in the learning you do on a daily basis. Ensure that you meet somebody new and understand their approach to investing; they may give you a slightly different perspective on your thoughts and plans – or they may have a slightly different, or more successful strategy for you to try.

- Go on another investment training course or programme to learn another skill. This may add a different slant to your existing skills, or replace them entirely. Please keep learning and developing.

- Take time to expand and nurture the group of people around you, and you will increase your own power and success. Surround yourself with the people you most want to be like.

Six-Monthly

- Check your personal credit records and credit score again to check what impact your investing activity has had on your credit score.

  If there are still items on your file since your first review that are not true, or that can be managed better, then take the appropriate action.

  Remember that your credit record is your responsibility, so manage it well. There are certain ways in which you can amend or limit information on your credit file, so contact the relevant credit agency or your Citizens Advice Bureau to find out how to do that.

- If all is well then continue to work your credit score and credit facilities to your advantage. It may well be time to get another credit card to give you another option on your investing, or it may be time to phone the credit card company and move your credit limit up (or interest rate down) again.

- Go back and review your notes from each training session you have attended – you will learn something or remember something new every time! Add to your notes on a constant basis and, after each separate training, go back and review your notes from all the other trainings you have done because your new perspective will add another dimension to previous information.

- Review each area that you invest in – or want to invest in – and check the basic criteria of **Take A RIDE** all over again. It is important that you do this as information and situations change rapidly and there could be some change that has occurred to one of the test criteria that would radically alter your investing decision. As a reminder, the criteria of **Take A RIDE** are:

  - **Actual evidence**: look at the real returns, the real rents and the real property activity in your chosen area.

  - **Ratio**: has the standard ratio moved, and if so has it got stronger or weaker? The ratio is the average salary for an area divided by the average property price in that exact same area.

    Remember when you are reviewing the ratio that the smaller the ratio number, the stronger the prices are in the property market you're looking at. Conversely, the bigger the ratio number, the weaker the market.

    A small number would be anything below three and a high number would be eight or above.

  - **Interest rates**: The lower the interest rate, the stronger the property market and the more likely that prices will be rising. So you can get a sense of the strength of the property market from this – as the governor of the Bank of England knows only too well.

    Review rates to determine whether to apply fixed or variable rates to your portfolio. If you think rates are going to rise then fixing now would seem to be an advantage, but if you think they will remain low then variable deals offer better profitability. But of course, if you are a very cautious investor then fixing your rates probably suits your personality better in any case.

- **Demand**: has demand for housing changed? The higher the demand, the higher the prices will go. Always remember to check this in conjunction with supply of housing stock. If supply is constant and demand increases, then prices must rise. If supply is constant and demand decreases then prices will fall.

  In the UK, demand far outstrips supply on a regular basis; however, please check the success or impact of the varying governmental strategies designed to alleviate this challenge. Also watch out for local initiatives.

- **Employment and Economics**: in times of high employment demand for housing increases – so when employment in your investment area is high, then property prices will be strong. Conversely, if employment is low and we have high unemployment, then demand for housing falls – because people feel that they can't afford to buy property – and prices weaken. And has the economy changed? Keep an eye on the GDP (Gross Domestic Product) to help assess the state of the economy at large.

Annually

Each year you need to:

- **Review your whole portfolio again.**

  Do this each and every year and drive up the returns on your investments to make your portfolio more and more productive for you. When you first start developing your portfolio, it is likely that you took on properties that had small profits, were perhaps close to breaking even, or were even loss-making.

To an extent, if it gets you started and you are happy with that, then that is fine. However, when your portfolio is fully invested – so say your plan was to get eight income-generating properties and two capital property projects and you now have that – then go back and review the whole lot with a more experienced eye.

So, let's say the eight income-generating properties are all positive, they wash their faces and produce returns of 5%, 6%, 7%, 8%, 9%, 10%, 12% and 15% respectively on your money invested. We start by reviewing the lowest performing property – i.e. the one generating the 5% return – to see what we can do.

Using a simple example, let's say this property generates £150 per month for you. In isolation this may seem fine but you should always ask if you could do better.

Now whether you are a newcomer to this or an experienced investor with a mature and complete portfolio you still need to constantly review what's going on.

So ask yourself:

- Can I get a higher rent?
- Can I get a cheaper – perhaps a discounted – mortgage?
- Can I get a better deal with the management company?
- Can I manage it myself now?
- Can I reduce my other costs by getting a group insurance deal or a better maintenance contract?

So, in our example, let's say that by reviewing all this we manage to drive up the income from this property from £150 to £173 per month and the return on our money goes up from 5% to 6.9%.

If we now pop those figures back into our list of properties and their returns we see that this one – which had been our worst performer – now isn't because we have driven the return up. Now, in this case, the property can stay and we now start reviewing and driving the next lowest – in this case the 6% return property – from our list and off we go again.

Let's say we can't improve the return at all and it stays at 6% – now we can make a decision and I suggest you now have this property on your potential sale list. I don't suggest you buy and sell too often, but have this one as a potential sale in your mind and then as soon as you find another property that would beat it – let's say you find a property that generates a 10% return – you now have the option to sell the six percenter, buy the ten percenter and thereby drive up the return from your whole portfolio.

If you did this regularly over time you can see that the returns from your portfolio would get higher and higher.

Now, even if you don't want to sell anything and you want to constantly expand your portfolio, this is still a good discipline and it focuses you on driving the returns up rather than becoming complacent with what you've achieved so far.

However, please make sure that you take account of the costs of switching properties in this way.

By constantly challenging the low performers you can see that investors with experience can consistently drive up the returns on their portfolios, so you would always expect an experienced investor to be getting higher returns than a novice; it makes sense.

Another benefit of doing this is that once the portfolio is fully invested, you have the opportunity to cherry-pick investments and only go for the high-producing ones – at that stage you have emotional and financial bargaining strength.

- **Do a tour of all your properties.**

  Touring your properties does many things: firstly, it reminds you of how much you have achieved – so have a look and celebrate your achievement! Secondly, it forces you to review the locality again. There may have been changes; for example, a new tower block being built at the end of the road or a major factory which may provide job opportunities – these are all factors which would change your opinion on the expected income or return on your investment.

  While you are there, take the time to go and say hello and thank you to all of your local power team – the managing agent, the builder and even the tenant. It might even be appropriate to take small gifts to your team to show your appreciation. Make sure you talk to them all – you never know what they may now know or what opportunities they are aware of that you would never spot living so far away.

  Happy touring!

- **Make sure that the strategy is still appropriate.**

  Does your strategy still work for you and your circumstances? We all go through different times in our life where our circumstances change. So keep reviewing your strategy to see if it's right for you and the people close to you. It would certainly change if you had a baby, won the lottery, had to fund children through university and so on.

It would be a total mistake – or a total miracle – if you were to keep the same strategy throughout your investing career, and it would suggest that you weren't generating the best returns.

So there we have it – some simple, time-based exercises for you to incorporate into your investing life to improve the returns and get better control of your money and your time.

Have fun!

FAQs

These are the most common questions I get from potential investors.

- **Has the market turned, then?**

  Although it's easy to think that the property market moves in one continuous motion, this isn't the case. We hear on the news and read in the newspapers that the market has risen or fallen by a certain percentage, but this is an average of all property movements over all areas.

  However, what actually happens is that there are hundreds of different movements – so houses might rise while flats fall; city centre flats might fall by more than seaside flats; big houses could rise more than small ones and houses in the south could rise by more than houses in the north.

  So, nothing happens **all together** in the property market and any one average figure is purely a combination of hundreds – or possibly thousands – of different underlying property movements.

  Therefore, not all property prices can move as one and consequently 'it', as in the market overall, cannot move in one direction, neither up nor down, in a single movement.

  Also, we can never identify the exact time it changes direction as an average – the market cannot possibly turn one way or another at a specific time, like 2.30 on a Thursday.

  So although we might, in retrospect, be able to identify the time one single property changed its price, the market itself can never 'turn' and it's a futile exercise looking for the moment it has turned or will in the future.

  It's much more important as an investor to look for a specific property and its potential to increase in value by studying the relevant information – which is possible to do – than it is to try and predict the market overall – which isn't.

- **Where shall I invest?**

  This is still the most common property-related question

I ever get and, of course, the answer isn't what people want to hear.

There is no one place – like 45 The High Street, Trumpton – that is the perfect investment opportunity.

The perfect investment place does not exist and nor does the perfect time.

A good investment is one that has one of the situations that we know will create a positive environment for investment added to the existence of customer demand for the property.

In short, the best place to invest isn't a place; it's a demand-driven situation.

Another answer is to say that the best place to invest is where it works for you and your business – which of course is different for all of us.

This is a flawed question.

What happens if the market falls?

There are several answers to this one, and most of them are variants of 'do nothing'.

But of course it does depend on why you bought a particular property. If you bought it for income, you should have made sure that it had a positive cash flow, in which case there will have been no change to that as a result of the fall (or in fact a rise) in property values.

The value of a property may go up and down (remember the wibble-wobble jelly?) and if your income property has hit a down period then my guidance is simple: don't sell it that day! The fall in the underlying value is only a problem for you if you realise that loss by selling the property during that period; so grit your teeth and don't sell it that day.

If you originally bought the property for capital gain then the challenge is different. However, it's likely that you calculated your original forecast figures with a profit for you and hopefully a contingency amount in there too.

If you did that, then it's likely that the property still works and would create a profit if you sold it now. However, if it doesn't work as a result of the drop in value, this may be the time to test out that second exit strategy and put a tenant in it and hold on to it for a time while the price recovers.

Other variations on 'Where's the best place and the best time?'

Oh dear – reread all previous answers.

Can you tell me how you really do it?

This is a weird one and I normally get this at the end of a long property seminar, sometimes lasting two or three days. After listening to all the evidence and formulae a person will whisper in my ear and say, "That's all very well, Gill, but how do you *really* do it?"

And of course the answer is: I use the evidence, formulae, knowledge and experience – there is no shortcut to being good at this. It takes graft, effort, application and all the other things I've written about in this book.

There isn't a magic bullet – I really do it like this!

Shall I buy my own home first or an investment property?

As usual there is more than one answer to this and it starts with some self-awareness, as I can't possibly tell you what to do here.

My experience though is this: if a person is in need of a nest or a home or wants to settle down (and I have to say that that's more likely to be a woman here), then getting your own home is the priority.

If, however, you are *not* ready to settle and are more driven by the property business, then getting some properties under your belt quickly can reap dividends in the future – you may even find that the investment properties generate the income you need to pay for your own home.

If you decide to go for investment properties when really your own home and nest is your priority then you won't be a good investor, since whatever property you're looking at, you will always secretly be thinking 'I wonder if I could settle in here?', and so you will be looking at the property more as a Dom or a Dora than as a Pete or a Pam.

Finally, if in any doubt, get your own home first as that will give you the secure base that you need to go forward in whatever you do.

I've got this fantastic property that was left to me by my aunt/I acquired when my partner left me/I picked up in a pub one night – insert your own scenario – but it doesn't cash flow. What shall I do?

I am constantly surprised by the amount of people that have a property lurking in their background for one reason or another and, in fact, most investors get started with these accidental or opportune acquisitions.

But however you acquired the property my suggestion is the same: while you are developing your property strategy and getting educated in this arena I suggest you leave the odd property you have on the back-burner and ignore it for a while.

Then, when your strategy is clear and you are getting started on your professional career, look again at the odd property; shake it down and analyse it as if it were a deliberate and professional purchase. If it passes all the tests you would now apply, then keep it and, if it doesn't, then consider getting rid of it.

Also, if it doesn't work, then go through the section on driving the return to see if you can make it work for you.

Again, if you can't make it work then that's one to consider letting go.

How much money do I need to start investing?

This is one of those 'how long is a piece of string' questions to which there is no real sensible answer because the answer is 'it depends'. It depends on your strategy, and chosen location; your purchasing method; whether you're going this alone or with some joint venture partners, etc.

So, in all honesty, if you're going to joint venture you can probably start with nothing (if you're putting in the sweat equity while the other person puts in the cash equity, for instance), or very little – say, £1,000 or so.

You could also get started by finding deals for others and, at Fielding Financial, we have a buddy board and deal swap facility to enable our students to get started with this.

You could then earn money from 'selling' the deal rather than doing the deal – and sourcing fees would be a couple of per cent of the purchase price. Do a few of those and you have enough money to get started on putting real money into deals.

If you want to put cash into a deal then aim to put as little as possible since we know from a previous section that the less in the deal, the higher the percentage return on our money. So, if you're buying a one-bed flat in Wigan costing £60,000, expect to put in approximately £15,000. If you're going to buy a one-bed flat in London expect to put in about £100,000!

Then you have some people who leave money in deals and some people who take it out – you can remortgage a property after six months and take out your money, as long as the property has increased in value of course, otherwise that tactic doesn't work (see the section on mortgages).

So even if you put in £15,000 today you could get it back in six months' time – so does that count?

Anyway, hopefully you get the gist – you can put in as little or as much as you want and if you only have a little money to start with (or even nothing), you need to start with different deals in a different way.

It depends!

CHAPTER 8

The Bigger Issues

To say I'm concerned about the state of UK housing is an understatement. The older I get, and the more I learn about it, all the more worried I become as I'm not terribly sure there's anyone doing much 'joined-up' thinking on many of the different, and pressing, issues involved in moving on from where we are.

As an aside, I just want to say how wonderful it is to be able to spend time thinking about these bigger issues; this opportunity only really comes about when you can stop worrying about how to pay the gas bill and feed the kids. Almost everybody I meet has bigger passions, missions and concerns: the state of the environment, or the NHS; religion or the homeless, and many want to 'save' something or other, to do good and to embark upon the journey of what's called 'giving back'. I personally don't like that term much as I never took anything in the first place, but hey-ho, we'll go with it for now.

My point here is this: it's only when you can feed and support your own family and yourself, and have some concrete idea of how to maintain your future financial security or freedom, that your mind can meander on to these bigger issues – so get there as soon as you can because that's when you can start making a difference by addressing these more national or global issues and, possibly, live a more purposeful and satisfying life.

Not everybody gets this bigger issue 'gig'; if you do, you'll broadly understand what I mean and if you don't then no worries, just fast forward to the next paragraph.

The Ticking Time Bomb in UK Housing

There are some radical and fundamental issues and challenges with UK housing, most of which are centred around the national demand and supply.

The Demonisation of Landlords

Nobody loves a landlord! Or at least, that used to be the case.

I have to admit that I've been abused by all sorts: tenants, the council, my so-called friends, colleagues and even by one national housing charity (who shall remain nameless here at least).

The housing charity I think was the most galling. One of my greatest pleasures now is the ability and opportunity to donate to charity. I like supporting charities, but the support and the charity has to mean something and be relevant to me. That's why housing charities spring to my mind as potential matches. After all, much of my money has been made from investing in UK housing; what better opportunity to support UK housing than by supporting homeless charities in the UK?

I met the then-Chief Executive on an ITV programme I made, just before Christmas 2007, called *Star Trader*. It was a programme that traded certain items, via a selection of celebrities, to create a valuable charity auction lot which was then auctioned live by Christopher Biggins; the show was hosted by Phillip Schofield.

The chosen charity set to receive the money was a large national housing charity and I was selected as the final contestant. My part in the show was to have a private cookery lesson with Marco Pierre White in return for donating to the cause something of substantial value. I decided to donate a selection of diamonds, which I had made into a beautiful set of jewellery: a necklace, earrings and a ring[4].

The TV show came and went and, a short time later, I was in the head office of the charity presenting a personal cheque for £25,000 to the Chief Executive and we planned for me to connect with the charity, and I did go and look at some of their projects. My intention was to donate every year and to become part of their support group – until I met a woman who was involved in running the charity.

4 If you ever get to see that programme you'll see the end result of all the work we did: the jewellery raised many thousands of pounds for charity. In fact, the final auction lot was bought by one person – a tall man; my husband. So in the end I got those diamonds back!

I wouldn't say she was a complete idiot but she did lack vision and she quickly put me off by treating me like the scum of the earth. To her, I was a private landlord and consequently their universal enemy. She viewed me so badly that I never went back and I've never given them a penny since and that's a terrible shame – not only for them but also for the hundreds of homeless people I could have helped.

Sadly the attitude of that, and similar charities, is that the private landlord is evil and, until that attitude changes, we are limiting the help we can give. You only have to read some of their offensive adverts to appreciate their view of the private landlord. If I had more time and energy for legal matters I would attempt to sue them for libel.

I'm not naïve: I understand that there are bad landlords out there – the amateurs who refuse to get educated and take any responsibility; those who put profit completely above people and any humane consideration. I get that. But personally I don't know any of those kinds of landlords. I've never met anyone like that in my forty years in this business. All I know are good, honest, decent folk making a reasonable living at what they do and enjoy.

But it isn't only charities that give us a hard time.

Many people think that running a business in property is evil. I'm not entirely sure why it's more evil to be a landlord than, say, a hat shop owner – they both sell products for money and profit – but people do. There's a natural assumption from many that we as a collective are about abusing people but I'm simply a business owner trying to do my best, and if I don't do my best my business isn't as successful as it can be.

Part of that success is my customers, the tenants. If I were bad at what I do then I wouldn't keep a tenant for longer than six months – and as I write I have one tenant who has been with me for almost thirty years. You can't keep a tenant or a customer that long without being pretty good at what you do.

So I have a better idea for all those organisations and people who think that landlords are the devil's work: why not work together?

There are failings on all sides here; there are certainly governmental failings, landlord failings and even charity failings. However, united we could make a difference; we could house the homeless and, in fact, my view is that the problem is so large that no one group can do this alone: we are only going to crack this problem if we all work together.

Let's implement landlord registration – I would welcome that with open arms, as it would take all the amateurs out of the marketplace.

Almost all professional landlords get some registration in any case. They need it for their HMO licences because professionals don't just do BTL; they do HMOs and other things too. Again, like any business, we have more than one type of property; more than one product or service on offer.

Let's discuss and negotiate a joint and successful solution: there is no one group or charity that is more empowered by this country to do this than I am; nor do they, or any housing charity, have any God-given right to occupy the moral high ground – because actually I'm already there!

We should *all* be attacking the amateur landlords who invest without knowledge, licence, responsibility or regulation. Let's work together to flush them out and have compulsory information.

But what we have to stop doing, and *now*, is tarring us all with the same brush.

I understand that charities and organisations mean well, but in many cases they're attacking the wrong people and, as you can probably tell from this rant of a section, I feel offended, abused and wrongly accused and I don't like that – and ultimately their stance has deprived them of all the money I intended to give. Now that can't be the solution they're after.

The Pensions Solution

Rather bizarrely, one of the most viable potential solutions to our housing crisis has arisen from the potential changes in our pension regulations, and it's at times like this that I think there may actually be someone senior in government thinking this through!

The Pensions Background

State pensions are a relatively new thing in terms of our country's history; they were a hundred years old in 2008, having been introduced by the Old Age Pensions Act on 1st August 1908.

To understand a little about the background of our state pensions system, and why we're in such a mess with it now, it's useful to go back and find out why the state pension was introduced in the first place.

And I'm afraid it comes down to politics and elections.

Now, I won't harp on about this as basically it's not going to help us going forward but the Liberals got elected in the UK in 1906 with a large majority of 397 seats to the Conservatives' 156, with Labour coming in a distant third with 29 seats.

However, as their electoral term progressed, the Liberals realised that their political support was failing and they had a pretty good idea that they would struggle to win the next general election, set for 1910.

And in fact they were right; they did win, but only by one seat – they had 272 to the Conservatives' 271.

So that's an interesting framework – a struggling political party who then embarked on a series of social reforms, partly because that was their policy, I guess, but also to try to hold on to political power.

The Pensions Act 1908 was consequently passed in that difficult time and many commentators believe that it was passed as no more than a piece of electioneering propaganda.

It's easy to believe that: there didn't actually appear to be any real evidence that there was any intention to pay out on this newfangled benefit because it was introducing a pension for anyone *over* the age of seventy at a time when the average life expectancy for men was slightly less than fifty years and for women only just over fifty.

In addition to that, the pension itself was means tested, *plus* you had to be of sound character and couldn't claim a pension if you had:

- Been in prison.
- Been a drunkard under the Inebriate Act 1898.
- Had a 'habitual failure to work'.

So there were many hurdles – both financial and, frankly, judgemental – placed in the way of people receiving this pension. As you can guess, not many people qualified!

So it does seem that this Act of Parliament was only passed as a piece of propaganda, an electioneering promise, and there never was any intention ever to pay out on it.

Subsequently, from 1908 until today, a variety of governments have been pushed into furthering this 'election promise' into something that is now tangible and real – and unworkable.

The sad thing is that the state pension was never intended to be payable on a large scale; it wasn't set up to be like that. Neither the infrastructure, nor the basic economics of a proposal, were ever planned or expected. The idea of a pension that supported you in your old age was probably nothing more than a false hope and a huge piece of bluff!

The Current Position

And from that inauspicious start we now find ourselves in the current day with a significant problem.

There are now eleven million pensioners, with more than 80% of the workforce living long enough to claim a pension. It is expected that there will be 12.5 million pensioners by the year 2025, when there will be only 3.5 working people for every pensioner compared to 4.5 now.

Now that is fundamental because the state pensions scheme hasn't been set up like a normal private pension scheme, where people pay in for a long period of time and the money gets invested and grows and that pot of money then provides a pension for the contributor.

Sadly, the government state pensions scheme is set up to enable the government to rob Peter to pay Paul, and the pensions for our current pensioners *today* are being paid for out of contributions in tax and National Insurance being made by the workforce *today*.

So, as the workforce diminishes and the population ages, we have a widening gap between what comes in and what needs to go out – so no wonder the government are changing the pensions law.

Pensions Solution

It is that series of changes that may partly rescue the UK housing situation because from April 2015 the majority of UK pensioners with a private fund of some kind will be able to withdraw their pension in its entirety and spend or invest it; and one of the most successful investments in the UK since the Domesday Book has been property.

Now wouldn't that be an elegant and perfect solution?

Property has always been seen partly as retirement potential. Many families retiring now realise that they've made more money from their property than they did working for a living, and that's an eye-opener. But the way that property can help in retirement is changing. In the past a couple could buy their first home in their twenties and then trade that up to larger and more valuable houses over time. By doing that for forty years or so it meant that the property pot was quite substantial.

If we take a notional £100k house that doubles every eight years – as is common in the UK – over a forty-year period that property would double five times to a staggering value of £3.2million.

Then, as the age of retirement comes along, they release the equity in some way, either through a mortgage or downsizing, to create a pot of money to live off.

But that option isn't really available to people retiring in the future because of the change in the age of the first-time purchaser. Now only 6% of properties are transacted by people under the age of thirty, and the average age of a first-time buyer is now well into the mid- and even late thirties.

Consequently, they have less time to trade up to larger and more valuable houses or to wait for their property asset to grow, such that when they get to their sixties and beyond, there is less equity in the property to release and live off.

Property Pensions

Many people have been using property to fund their retirement for some time now. Although not technically a pension in the formal sense, it can serve the same purpose in that property can give a regular monthly income, plus lump sum 'withdrawals' at given times.

There are several advantages to creating your own private retirement fund in this way:

- The fund – or portfolio – of property is totally within your own control.

- There are no legislative or regulatory restrictions as to how that property is handled, so the owner can take money regularly from that property, or not, as they wish and the only limitation is the property itself and the cash it generates.

- Many people feel more comfortable with investing their future money in something they understand, like property, rather than in the more traditional pensions investments, which are shares, or equities, often in managed funds.

Therefore increasingly people are looking at using property as the investment to fund their retirement. Many people are already doing this, and many more are likely to start as a result of changes in pension legislation in 2015.

NB: investment in residential property is not currently an allowable investment *within* standard pension funds, and there is no indication that there will be any change to this restriction in the future.

Pensions 2015

There are many changes that happened to pensions in April 2015; the main one we are concerned with here is the ability to withdraw *all* funds from an existing formal pensions fund without any limits or restrictions.

Obviously, if your intention is to create a property-based retirement fund then access to this money could provide all the seed capital you need to get started. Under the new legislation, the entire existing pension fund can be withdrawn if:

- You are old enough – currently fifty-five, but this will be increasing in the future.
- You have an SIPP or other personal pension.
- You have a workplace pension that is a defined *contribution* scheme.

Workplace Pensions

There are two main types of workplace or job-based pensions: the defined contribution (DC) scheme and the defined benefit (DB – otherwise known as the final salary) scheme.

If you have a defined contribution scheme you will receive a pension based on what the contributions are worth at the time. In this case, all the contributions you, and possibly your employer, have made have been put into a pot and invested on your behalf. So what you get as a pension depends on the amount put in, plus investment returns and less fees and charges made by the fund managers.

However, with a defined benefit scheme you will receive a pension based on a predetermined benefit – and in most cases this will be a final salary scheme which is calculated on, for example, your final year's salary or an average of recent salaries; but the issue here is that you will be able to calculate this pension figure in advance because the benefit is already defined.

For workplace pensions then, if you have a defined *contribution* scheme you may withdraw all of your money in one go, but if you have a defined *benefit* scheme you may not.

If you do have a defined benefit scheme and you want to withdraw it all, the route to take is to transfer that pension into a personal pension and then withdraw from there; however, this is probably *not* a good thing to do as defined benefit schemes are generally very good.

If you are considering this then please seek professional financial advice.

The Process of Withdrawal

If you decide that you do wish to withdraw all of your pension fund in one go, all you need to do is to contact your pension fund administrator or Pension Trustee. You will find their contact details on any pension correspondence you have received.

However, be careful – these withdrawals will be liable for tax!

The Tax Issue

Firstly, the good news: the first 25% of any pension fund withdrawal is always tax-free.

However, whatever you withdraw beyond that 25%, you will pay tax on it at your standard rate. So you would pay tax on the remaining 75% whatever the pension is – therefore it makes sense *not* to withdraw it all in one go as that would almost certainly put most people into higher rate tax. The logical approach would be to withdraw in phases to keep personal income or earnings in the lower tax rates, which are as follows:

Income Tax Rates and Taxable Bands for 2016–2017

Rate	2016–2017
Basic rate 20%	£0–£32,000
Higher rate 40%	£32,001–£150,000
Additional rate 45%	Over £150,000

Simple Illustration

At the end of every tax year (which runs from 6th April in one year to 5th April the following year), a person's tax liability is calculated by adding up all their income from all sources for that tax year, which could include a job, property rental income, interest from savings plus that received from a pension.

That comes to a total of, let's say, £101k. The person then deducts their personal allowance, which for those born after 5th April 1948 is £11,000 (2016/2017), and they can also deduct any other allowances and deductions as appropriate.

If we assume that creates a total of:

£101,000 – £11,000 = £90,000

The resultant tax bill would be as follows:

The first £32,000 @ 20% tax = £6,400, then
The remaining (£90,000–£32,000) £58,000 @ 40% tax = £23,200
Total tax is therefore £23,200 + £6,400 = £29,600

So you can see that the more you withdraw, the more likely you'll be in the 40% or even the 45% tax rate band.

NB: figures are for illustration purposes only and are not representative of any one individual's tax liability. Please seek financial guidance in respect of personal tax liability.

Taxation rates and allowances may change each year. Figures, rates and allowances used are for the tax year 2016–2017 only.

Summary

In essence then, there is nothing magical about to happen in respect of property and pensions. Some people have always used property as their retirement fund and many people have been able to use their pension fund as seed capital to build a property portfolio if they choose.

The only real issue to be aware of is the tax to be paid on funds withdrawn, and it makes sense to plan this carefully to ensure that the minimum tax is paid overall.

Further Information

Further information can be found from:

- A financial advisor.
- The pension administrator, or Pension Trustee, of any pension scheme.
- Websites such as: www.pensionsadvisoryservice.org.uk or www.moneyadviceservice.org.uk

The Property Future

My personal view is that the time of the property investor is now. I have noticed that for me personally I am increasingly being invited to speak at, or attend, more senior or high profile events and meetings than ever before. As a long-standing and experienced investor I am being asked to present the view of the property investor. And that reflects the attitude of the world at large. Local authorities are becoming friendlier towards us, and so is the government, because they need our properties to provide the nation's accommodation and so help with resolving some of our social issues, for instance, by housing the homeless. Combine that with the enormous number of property shows on the TV and the number of people investing and we have a bit of a positive groundswell going on.

So what would the property investor of the future tell us about trends and events impacting us? Here are my top seven predictions for the property investing future.

- There will be, at some stage, investor regulation. As privately provided housing increases further the government will have to act to get the amateurs and accidental landlords out of this profession and so there will be some form of licencing and regulation for property investors – and that can't come a moment too soon for me.

- Local authority housing will decline even further and local councils will increasingly use private landlord-provided property for their needs. In eighteen years' time my prediction is that approximately half of all property will be owner occupied with the remaining half being split, with 40% provided by professional investors and the remaining 10% by housing associations, housing charities and local authorities.

- We will increasingly become like mainland Europe in our attitudes to housing, with home ownership being regarded more as a business thing and less as a personal thing. Property ownership will be part of pension provision and included as a major part in overall investment strategies for the individual, with shares becoming less important.

- As our population ages, there will be a change in demand with the rise of specific accommodation for seniors in the form of upmarket developments with onsite support or care and hotel-type housing for retirees. Overall, our housing demand, and consequently provision, will become more specific and tailored to its eventual user, with property for retirees, young families, students, pod-type accommodation for casual users and so on. So pick your investment niche now and start planning for it.

- Property ownership will become an old person's game, with fewer young people buying properties, and the age of the first-time buyer will be over forty.

- Funding for property purchase will become more flexible and commercial, with significant amounts of funds being provided by personal pensions schemes, private lending and crowd-funding-type arrangements.

- Properties on high ground will start to attract premium prices as we become increasingly concerned about global warming, flooding and environmental issues. So get ahead of the crowd on that one and add a 'feet above sea level' criteria to your property purchasing list.

So those are my seven predictions for future changes, but I know one thing that time or the future won't change, and that is the relentless upwards trend in property prices.

With demand still rising at about double supply at best, I cannot see any change in how our property prices continue to move up. Sadly, I believe that will take home ownership away from the masses and the norm and will take it increasingly into the preserve of the professional investor.

And as I sit here thinking about all that has happened up to the end of 2014, eighteen years after the introduction of buy-to-let, and looking forward to the next eighteen years of investing, I laugh at the absurdities of those early days, admire the efficiencies of today's investors, and look forward to the professionalism of property investing in the future.

Action Plan

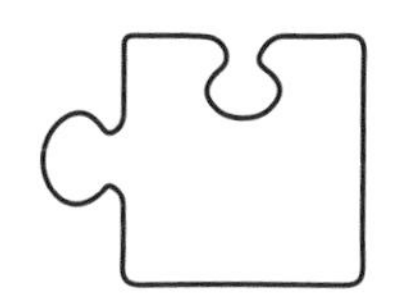

CHAPTER 9

The Whole Caboodle

Well here we are then, at the most important chapter – how to *really* do this property investing.

Now I do feel a bit mean because I didn't tell you at the beginning of the book that there was a section that pulled it all together; but if I had you wouldn't have read all the important stuff in between page one and here; and if you hadn't, then you wouldn't really get this part.

So I did it for your own benefit – it was tough love.

We have learned some important lessons in the book so far. Fundamentally, we have discovered that property investing isn't quite what we thought and it isn't done quite in the way we thought!

That's why I included the FAQs – because if you're *not* currently a property investor, the things you want to ask and are worried about are:

- Which location is best?
- How much money do I need?
- Isn't the market scary when it goes down?

Now that's Dom and Dora thinking (remember them, the residential purchasers? You see, I told you that you needed to read the bits in between!). These are questions and fears that rightly bother the residential purchaser because they are important for Dom and Dora.

However, they're not in the main the issues that bother Pete and Pam, our professional property partners, because they're not important for them. Why?

Pete and Pam are in this as a business and they concern themselves with business issues like:

- Business planning (strategy).

- Customers and demand for their product.

- Cash flow.

Different. A different set of concerns approached in a different way and, honestly, if you don't get that then this book needs to become your latest doorstop and nothing else. But I hope by now that you do, more or less, get that.

Of course, both Dom and Dora and Pete and Pam are active in the same marketplace and obviously there are overlaps: so Dom and Dora want to live by a good school and that piece of information creates demand for our product so Pete and Pam are interested in the school too, but the interest is from a different perspective.

Dom and Dora are interested because they want the best for their children: Pete and Pam are interested because they *know* that what Dom and Dora and other residential buyers want creates the demand for their business product. So some parts of property investing look quite similar to the residential purchasing view, but some look quite different.

Dom and Dora probably don't like run-down areas; Pete and Pam quite like that because it suggests there's an opportunity to increase value.

Dom and Dora tend not to like it when the property market goes down in value; Pete and Pam (if they've done their strategy right) don't mind because:

- It creates demand for rental properties. Because Dom and Dora don't buy when the market goes down they rent instead, thereby creating demand for Pete and Pam's rental product.

- If Pete and Pam have set up their rental properties properly then the property washes its face and provides a good ROCI, so what do they care if the market goes down, and why would they want to sell an asset that's creating money for them? The only issue is the sales value, so I have a tip there – *don't sell it that day!* Don't sell the property until the market comes back up – as it always does. Remember the Domesday Book story?

- If Pete and Pam have CPs, or B&Fs, they would have built some contingency into their projects to allow for price fluctuations and they would always have done the Wash its Face income check in addition to their second strategic option. Again, if the price has fallen too far, and below their contingency buffer, then they would rent the property out instead.

Professional Investor's Tip

I just wanted to add a tip here from a well-known wealth creator, Warren Buffet. Now we have to accept that he knows a thing or two about markets in general and his philosophy is this: if I'm a net buyer of any asset, then I always want the price to be falling (because overall the net price of acquisition is less). Of course when he's a net seller of his asset *then* he wants the price to be rising – so wait for that to happen.

Summary

Property investing is different to residential property purchasing; we need to learn that difference and adapt to the change in perspective that results from that understanding.

And the fundamental issues are: there is no perfect place to invest – that doesn't exist and, in any case, what may be a perfect-looking place today may not be a good place tomorrow; looking for the perfect location geographically is a fool's errand. The best place in which to invest isn't a geographical place; it's a circumstance – *demand!*

Furthermore, there's no perfect amount to invest. That has to be a function of the amount you have, the place you go, your attitude to risk, your personal circumstances, the strategy you're working and the deals you do, both with properties and with people.

Now, if you promise me that you do broadly get that, then we can now look at how I do it!

The Seven-Step Plan to Investing

Step One: the Idea

At this stage, we're not specifically looking at an individual property, but we are looking for an initial concept of potential. Some ideas, then, are:

- To look for an area of potential demand such as:
  - A university, college or hospital.
  - A large local employer.
  - A government intervention such as a planned road, railway or airport.
  - A retail or leisure development being announced.
- To follow up on a lead given to you by another investor, an agent or one of your friends or family.
- To look again at an area in which you already hold property.
- Plonk a pin in a map and start checking that area out.
- Follow up on news about the property market.

And I'm going to take that last one, an announcement of news, and start with the newspaper article we had at the beginning.

The Telegraph, **Wednesday 31st December 2014**

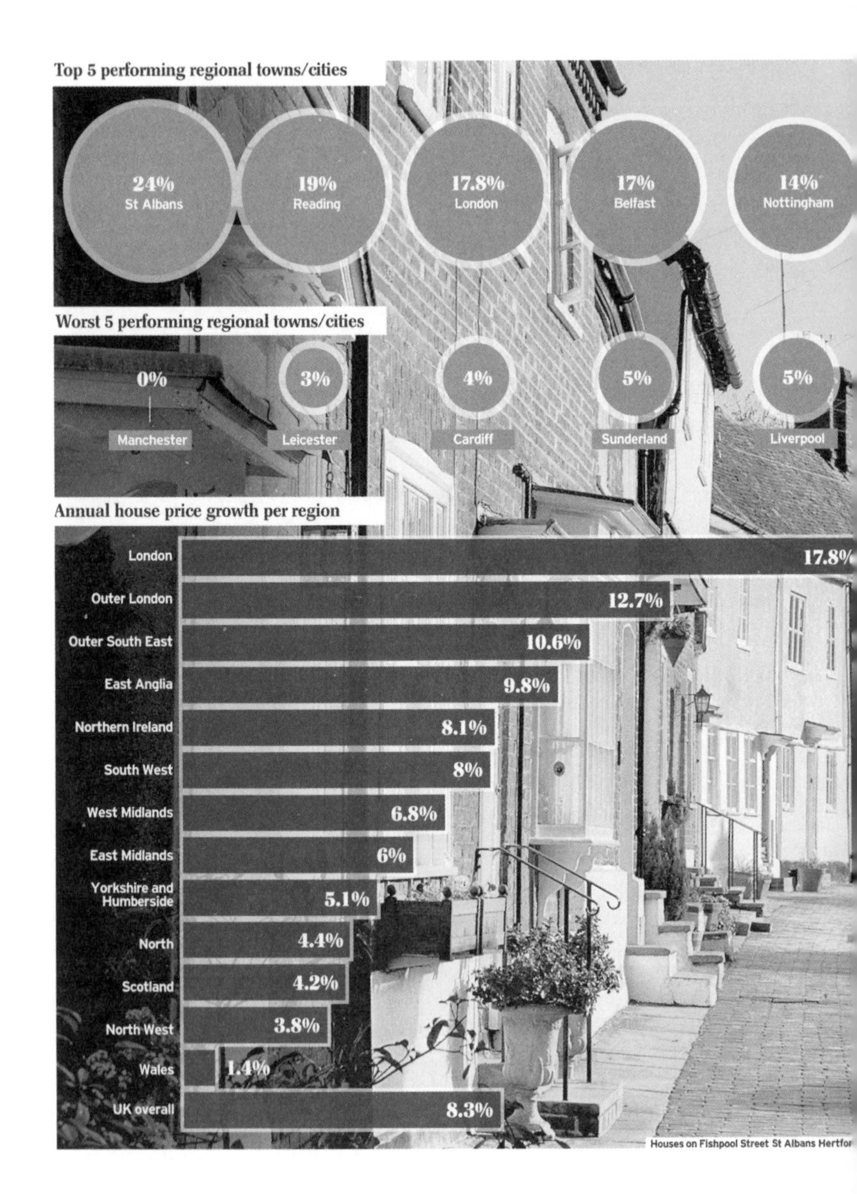

Houses on Fishpool Street St Albans Hertfor

Step Two: Consider the Opportunity

The thought here is to worry at the idea like a dog with a bone and pull it apart. Now, forgive me for repeating here but it saves you flicking back and forth (this is a repeat of one of the pages from Chapter 1): the things that I immediately pick up in reading these articles are:

- Manchester was our top performing price rise city in 2013, when the published price rise was 20% over the year, and now for 2014 it's the worst performing city at 0%! I would immediately go and look at Manchester to check all the other parts of Take A RIDE to see if it has overcorrected and is in line for a mini surge.

- I would try and workout why Reading and St Albans had done so well, and I can save us all time here and say it's to do with railways: London Crossrail is being extended out to Reading, while the north-south tranche of that is going north of London. Now that makes logical sense to me and I can probably conclude that those areas have had their big uplift and ignore them for the short term.

- I can start to highlight areas I will look to for potential investment, and what I do there is:

  - Ignore anything that had a big uplift in 2014, as it is unlikely that it will be a top performer in 2015.

  - Look for longer-term trends by comparing against prior years to see if an area is on a slow but relentless move up.

  - Take the average movement for 2013 – the 8.3% – and then delve deeper into those areas which underperformed that figure last year. I would check if there was any other evidence to suggest that it might underperform, or perhaps more likely overperform, the average in the following year.

So that highlights for me the potential areas that all increased less than 8.3%, which are:

- Northern Ireland
- South West
- West Midlands
- East Midlands
- Yorkshire and Humberside
- North
- Scotland
- North West
- Wales

I read all that and think it through and decide to take the North West as an area to look at because the area as a whole only rose by 3.8%, so low in comparison to the average, and it also includes Manchester which is intriguing me as it was top performer in 2013, had 0% growth in 2014 and looks right for a growth in 2015, *and* it is in the North West.

You can make any extrapolation from your ideas and thoughts you like – at this stage it's all still theoretical and we wouldn't be going to Manchester yet; we're still evaluating. But the moment an area or an idea fails to work, ditch it and go back again and get another one to work with.

Step Three: Narrow it Down

Now start working on the idea and rattling it about. So check things like the ratio – again repeated here from Chapter 1:

The North	3.4
Scotland	3.5
Yorkshire	3.7
North West	3.7
Northern Ireland	3.9
Wales	4.0
East Midlands	4.3
West Midlands	4.5

The North West, at 3.7, is below the national average so again I am satisfied and keep looking.

And at this stage I will start to focus in on an area or two – and I get a map of Manchester and the surrounding area looking for communications, motorways and layout.

From these two maps I decide that I'm going to (more or less randomly) look at one area west, one north and one east, within the Greater Manchester area. I specifically avoid the south, as that's where all the big news was in 2013 because it was connected with the Manchester Airport development project. I make a rough assumption at this stage that the south has had its big movement and leave it alone – although I can go back and check later. From the two maps, and my thoughts so far, I am going to pick three areas, then, and they are:

- Oldham (west).
- Wigan (west).
- Bolton (north west).

I then go and scout about for information on each area. It's important to note that you must use the same source if you're doing this comparison of area against area, otherwise you could be comparing apples with pears. In this instance, I use the Zoopla analysis of areas, and I get information about all three from that one consistent source.

Here's Oldham:

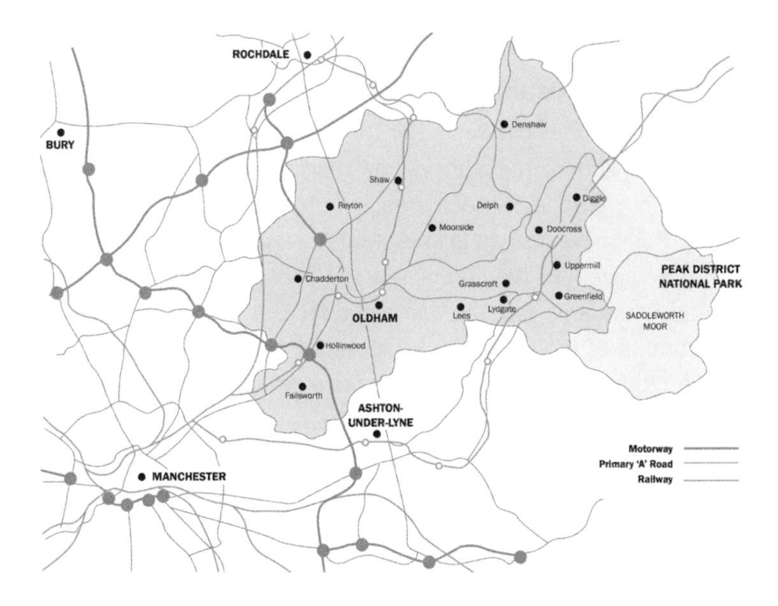

Asking price in Oldham

Property Type	1 bed	2 beds	3 beds	4 beds	5 beds
Houses	£90,627	£96,663	£148,129	£263,506	£414,083
Flats	£113,737	£169,487	£119,967	-	-
All	£104,750	£102,838	£147,900	£263,506	£414,083

Asking rents in Oldham

Property Type	1 bed	2 beds	3 beds	4 beds	5 beds
Houses	£562 pcm	£476 pcm	£533 pcm	£598 pcm	£550 pcm
Flats	£460 pcm	£482 pcm	£592 pcm	-	-
All	£505 pcm	£477 pcm	£535 pcm	£598 pcm	£550 pcm

Now, at this stage of the analysis I know nothing so I decide what route to take – income or capital – and select income (again, it doesn't matter which route you take as you evaluate it all ways eventually).

Rents Per Thousand (Pounds) Invested: RPK

The first test I do is the Rents Per Thousand invested (RPK) as this gives me a generic measure of how much rent, on average, I can earn from my money in each area.

RPK is calculated as follows: rent (this can be done either on the monthly rent or the annual rent – it doesn't matter as long as you use the same formula each time for comparison) divided by the number of thousands or Ks invested. I use monthly rent but it's fine to use annual rent – just make sure you compare like with like.

Using Oldham's figures for **all** one-bed properties (flats and houses), taken from the previous chart: £505/£104.75 = £4.82. So for every thousand invested I could earn £4.82.

Professional Investor's Tip

Over time, I have realised that RPK decreases with size of property – so the highest RPK will always be on the cheapest, smallest investments, and it gets smaller as the property gets larger.

Therefore, as I want my RPK overall to be as high as possible, I always start with assessing the smaller properties and only go for the larger ones if there's a specific demand or reason to do so.

Continuing the illustration for Oldham: for one-bed, two-bed, three-bed and four- and five-beds we get RPKs of £4.82, £4.62, £3.61, £2.26 and £1.32, which is a normal trend for properties – as the properties get bigger, the RPK gets smaller! So for each area I then do a more detailed calculation separating out flats from houses. If I look at the individual property types I get:

One-bed flats: £460/£113.737k = £4.04
One-bed houses: £562/£90.627k = £6.20
Two-bed flats: £482/£169.487k = £2.84
Two-bed houses: £476/£96.663k = £4.92

I put that on a chart – and do the same for Wigan and Bolton. I add all the figures to my table, which now looks like this:

	1 House	2 House	1 Flat	2 Flat
Oldham	£6.20	£4.92	£4.04	£2.84
Bolton	£3.73	£4.73	£5.50	£5.02
Wigan	£4.95	£4.88	£5.75	£4.78

And from this I can pick an area to focus on. We would perhaps assume that we go for one-bed houses in Oldham as that gives us the highest RPK overall at £6.20, but that's not my choice here because I like the trends to be regular and normal and predictable. Odd peaks and troughs can sometimes be an indication of other factors.

So my selection criteria would eliminate:

- Areas where the RPK varies too much.
- Odd peaks and troughs.
- Trend anomalies.
- High property prices – as a guide spend less, not more!

Therefore I discard:

- Oldham – because the peak at £6.20 is too high and there's a big variation from one end to the other at £2.84.

- Bolton – because, again, there's a big variation from the high at £5.02 and the low at £3.73, and there's a trend anomaly since the RPK from a two-bed house is higher than that for a one-bed house – that's not a normal trend.

- This leaves me to focus on Wigan!

Step Four: Start Looking for Specifics

We now need to find some properties to test as potential purchases. We know a bit about Wigan and we generally start at the bottom of a pyramid unless we have a reason not to. Therefore we start looking for a cheap and cheerful buy-to-let property in Wigan that would fit into our pyramid, our portfolio and our investment strategy.

I go to any generic property website and put in the required criteria, in this case:

- The place – Wigan.
- I exclude any other place – so just Wigan.
- Size – one- and two-beds.
- Look for flats.
- Don't worry about price at this stage – set that to nil.

Then click 'search' and see what arrives.

When I did this I saw lots of one-bed flats for between £45,000 and £55,000.

I also do a rental search, on the same website for the same place and so on, and I confirm rental values. In this case, one-bed flats rent for approximately £375 per month and two-bed flats rent for approximately £525 per month.

Now I do a rough Wash its Face calculation comparing two properties. In this case it's a one-bed flat for sale at £47,500 and a two-bed flat for sale at £49,950.

Running the numbers using a standard 75% Loan to Value interest-only mortgage at 5% per annum interest I get the monthly mortgage amounts, and I then add 10% of the rent allowance for the management fee and another 10% allowance for other costs (this isn't real but it will do as an approximation for now), and I get:

	One-bed	Two-bed
Rent	£375	£525
Mrtge (75% LTV 5% IO)	£148	£156
Mgt 10% + 10% OOE	£75	£105
Monthly surplus	**£152**	**£264**

Based on the estimated monthly cash surplus of £264, the two-bed wins at this stage.

However, I keep going and now calculate the Return On my Cash Invested (the ROCI) as follows:

	One-bed	Two-bed
Surplus	£152	£264
Investment: 25%	£11,875	£12,487
ROCI		
(surplus x 12/investment) x 100	**15.4%**	**25.3%**

I then factor in the exact RPK (rent/property price in Ks) and I get:

	One-bed	Two-bed
Surplus	£152	£264
Investment: 25%	£11,875	£12,487
ROCI	15.4%	25.3%
Total money invested	£47,500	£49,950
RPK (per month)	**£7.89**	**£10.51**

My decision at this stage is that I would rather have the two-bed, and that's because the RPK is higher, the ROCI is higher and the cash flow is higher. I make that decision even though my outlay is higher – i.e. the property is more expensive.

Now, I would check that as it might be that there's no demand for two-bed flats and so on but, for now, we'll take that as our choice.

Step Five: Check the Rest

What I would do now is to check the rest and if I have evaluated for income, as here, I would check the chosen property against **UPWARDS** to make sure that its capital value is solid and hopefully has the potential to grow.

The first part of **UPWARDS** is the area, and the first place to start with that is the UDP. You find those by looking on the web as follows: www.[your chosen area].gov.uk.

So Wigan would be: www.wigan.gov.uk.

We learn that there is an economic framework in place in the area which has plans for both self-employment, entrepreneurial opportunities plus employment growth.

That gets a tick from me.

I would also check communications and the motorway links around Manchester and see where they're going in terms of job opportunities.

And I can see that the motorways in the north and west go to Liverpool, Preston, Blackburn and Blackpool, and I might do some **Take A RIDE** checks there; but that's unlikely in this case as we have found so much already in Wigan and the surrounding areas.

I would do the same the other way, and to the east there is motorway access to Huddersfield, Halifax and Leeds and beyond.

I also check the railways for the same thing. Firstly, check an overall rail map. So let's look at the Northern Hub. Log on to www.networkrail.co.uk/improvements/northern-hub/.

What can we see? I can see immediately that there is a good network of stations and routes out of Manchester and, as before with the roads, in all directions out to Liverpool and Leeds, etc.

But then I get specific with public transport and find the train times (both the duration and specific times) from Wigan to Manchester city centre.

I discover that the train times are approximately forty to fifty minutes and that an Anytime Day Return ticket costs £9.30.

Now that sounds a lot to me initially, so I would then compare property prices just to make sure it's worthwhile spending forty-five minutes on a train each day going into central Manchester for work.

I discover that using the same analysis as I did before from Zoopla, so that I'm comparing like with like. I see that the prices in Manchester city centre are approximately double those in Wigan.

One-bedroom flats in Manchester are an average of £123,722 versus £64,231 in Wigan (at the time of writing), so it is quite likely to be worth travelling forty-five minutes a day to get into a better property; and for the commuter here, they can get a three-bed property in Wigan for the same price (both purchase and rental) as a one-bed in Manchester.

Rents in Wigan for a three-bed property are £514 per month and a one-bed in Manchester is £542, and comparing like with like, we can see that rents in central Manchester are about £200 per month more than Wigan.

From all that, I conclude that the U in **UPWARDS** gets a good 'tick' and I decide to continue reviewing the opportunity.

And from then on we can't really check any more of **UPWARDS** until we have a specific property to run it against – so leave that part until then.

Step Six: Check A RIDE

Now go back and check the overall area – in this case Wigan.

- **A**ctual evidence – checked that throughout.
- **R**atio: checked at the beginning – in the range of 3.50 to 3.73.
- **I**nterest rates low!
- **D**emand and supply – look for evidence of housing supply and demand. On www.placenorthwest.co.uk, for example we find something suggesting that Wigan is the same as any other place in the UK: demand outstrips supply.

  On 24th January 2014 Place Northwest published an article online which contained details of Wigan Council's plans to host a meeting to discuss a shortfall in new homes in the area.

  But then test that evidence by placing a specific advert for a tenant in the local paper, to check the demand is strong.

- Finally the E in Take A RIDE stands for Employment and the local Economy, and we already have some evidence from the business plan within the UDP; but again, just as a check, go on to a search engine and really look for a job! If work is plentiful then demand will be high.

Look for quality of jobs and salary ranges as well as the quantity of jobs available.

Step Seven: Decide and then Sort Out the Finance!

Assuming everything comes back in order, we are now ready to make the decision whether to buy or not. At this stage we look to sort out the money because now we have all the facts, figures, evidence and statistics available to enable us to make that decision in an informed way – up until now it's purely been guesswork!

What we have gone through, broadly, is the Evaluation Figure of Eight.

Evaluation Figure of Eight

As a guide, evaluate potential deals with the Evaluation Figure of Eight, which looks like this:

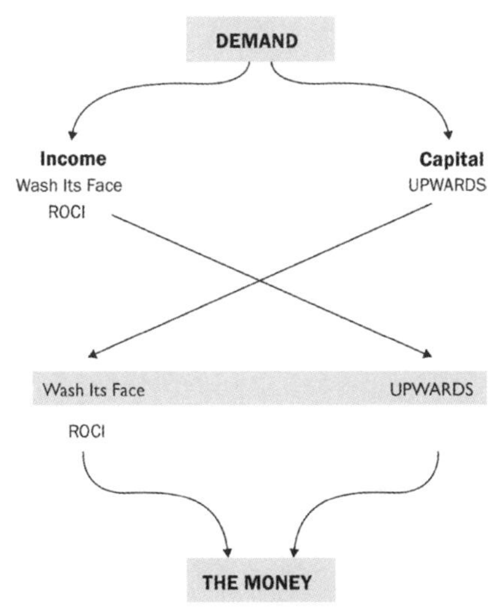

I start by identifying my *demand*, because there's no point doing any evaluation if there's no demand – if you don't have that please don't buy the property!

Then: I quickly identify whether, broadly, I think the property will fit into the capital part or the income part of my pyramid. It doesn't really matter, as I evaluate all properties for all things eventually anyway, but it gives me the ability to sift out the no-hoper more quickly. Then: If it's an income property, I evaluate the two important things first:

- **Does it wash its face – does it cash flow?**
- **What's the return on my money (ROCI)?**

Any that fails to hit my income target get rejected and I stop there. Or: If it's a capital property, I run it against the seven criteria of UPWARDS. Any that fail to hit my capital target get rejected.

Then, I swap those two over and:

- I check the capital ones for their potential to have a tenant, the cash flow and the ROCI.
- I check the income ones against UPWARDS to check their potential for capital gain.

I obviously do this reverse check to make sure I've protected my position and can see two potential exits from this deal, swapping from one to the other if the market changes or if I get stuck and the deal doesn't work as I anticipate. Then, and only ever then:

Step Eight

I work out how I'm going to pay for it.

Yes, that's right. I never, ever bother to check the money I need until this stage because I don't know enough to make a financial assessment.

Think about it. If someone came up to you and said, "I have a great property, it's worth £120,000 and you can have it for £100,000", would you take it? I hope not, and if you would please go back and start this book again!

We would need to assess it and see if it fits our strategy and so on. But let's assume it would fit our strategy and we now have a clean property sitting there. We now need to check if it would cash flow, and we need to check UPWARDS and the ROCI to get the information we need in order to work out if it's worth the money *to us*, and then to see if it works financially.

So, let's say you can get 100% funding at 5% from a source – an angel or a partner or even a standard mortgage. If the deal has an ROCI of 6% or above then it's worth the money to us because the funding costs would be covered; that's a positive proposition.

If, however, our funding costs us 10% then any deal generating less than that doesn't work and we should reject it.

It dumbfounds me why the amateurs work out whether they can afford it *before* they know what 'it' is and what the deal comprises. That's clearly daft because it's only when you know the detail of the deal that the affordability check makes sense. Otherwise it would be like running into a bank with £1,000, throwing it on the counter and running for the door. The bank teller would shout at you to come back and ask:

- What's it for?
- Do you want it on deposit or in a current account?
- Do you want instant access?
- Do you want to tie this in for a long time and get a higher rate of interest?
- Do you want to put it in an ISA?

In short, the bank teller will want to know what the money is doing and what are the terms and conditions of your deposit.

The same is true for property – you can't just throw money into the market without knowing the terms and conditions of the investment and understanding what you aim to do and why.

Crucial Tip

An experienced investor will tell you that if you find a good enough deal then the money will find you!

The Chute of Shame

(You have to say that in a Tower of Terror-type voice.)

Hopefully you're now comfortable enough for me to show you this – which is exactly how most amateurs do their evaluation and, consequently, how you are *never* going to do it.

What amateurs do – rather than the Evaluation Figure of Eight – is fall down the Chute of Shame, which looks like this:

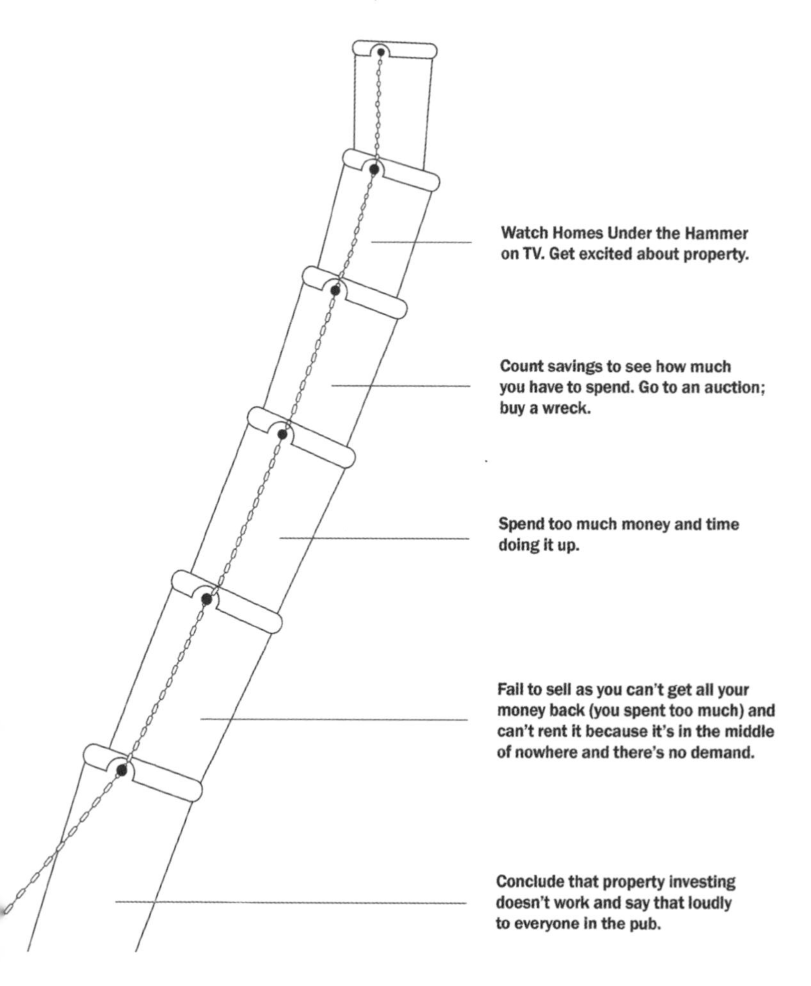

Summary

What we have done here is to check the validity of a newspaper article and to test if we could get a property investment from the idea it generated – and we can! Or at least I could at the time of writing, so please don't just go barging into Wigan on the day you read this as this evidence may not apply then – this is an academic exercise only and not a piece of investment advice!

If the analysis didn't work at any stage we could just go back and start again with a different area, sub-area or idea and off you go again.

The beauty of it is that it is formulaic!

At no stage have we discussed whether we *like* a property or not (because it doesn't matter); all we have done is to go logically through a series of well-trodden steps that will help us to identify a good deal and a good investment over a bad one.

It's unemotional and, to an extent, mathematical, and the numbers will tell you if the investment is right! There's no angst or sleepless nights – it's just a simple yes or no based on the evidence you find and the numbers you calculate.

Other Issues

In order to properly evaluate any property you need to set some targets for achievement, otherwise you won't know if it's a good deal or not, so here are some tips:

- For capital strategies, set yourself a target of 10% per strand of UPWARDS you get. So, for straightforward capital properties, 10% would be a minimum – i.e. one strand of UPWARDS.

- For B&Fs, half that is OK (i.e. 5%) as long as you're going to drop it into an income tier of your pyramid. But if it's a straight-in-and-out capital deal, then the 10% guidance would apply!

- For income, always compare the return for the property to what you could get elsewhere and, at the moment, that's pitifully low – the average savings rate is about 0.5%.

- For both strategies, add in the cost of your funding – again, that's very low at the moment but make sure your return is at least double the borrowing rates. So, if you're borrowing at 4% set a target return of 8%.

- Increase your target as you get more experienced and more successful. Perhaps increase your targets by 1% per property deal, or 1% per year of experience, so while it's fine to set an initial target of, say, 10%, that should be increasing to 40–50% or more once you've been doing this a few years.

AND FINALLY, HERE ARE THE REAL CRUNCH POINTS:

- Don't invest in property unless you are capable of evaluating the issues on Take A RIDE.
- Don't invest in property unless you really, *really* get the difference between Dom and Dora and Pete and Pam.
- Get yourself a property purchasing checklist with the relevant 'yes' and 'no' points for you.
- When creating your business plan, set your strategy properly to minimise risk.
- UPWARDS works! So use it!
- Make sure you have a complete toolbox of knowledge and experience and a connection to others, some with similar and some with better knowledge than you.
- Remember: the only measure that really matters is the return on your cash!

So go and invest. Be safe, professional and profitable!

Oh...and finally, I just wanted to say... **That it's been fun**.

I've been a property investor for nearly forty years and overall, it's been fun. There have been ups and downs of course but I'm still here and still going and investing. The deals are different now; I started with a small rental property in Burgess Hill that I bought, mainly for cash, after working flat out for over a year so I could 'save up' the deposit, and then borrowing the rest of the money on a mortgage.

My most recent deal is a small development of flats – being done with three other people – where we are borrowing 100% of the money from a private investor because it makes business sense to do so.

In between those two deals, I have seen every crazy and brilliant scheme the market has created: reversionary properties; sale and leasebacks; repossessions and buy and rent back; lease options; back to backs and joint ventures. I have bought properties for cash, on credit cards, with 100% mortgages and for no money down at all.

Financing options nowadays are more restrictive in some ways, but are better because the professional investor now does financial deals that are more collaborative, and I like that. Rather than formal mortgages, we are now more likely to use peer-to-peer funding, private investment, angel funding and short-term bridging finance.

My first property deal took me three years to complete: to buy, live in, rent out and sell, and since then, I have done much larger deals in three hours!

Along the way I have also bought all the standard stuff: BTLs, HMOs, B&Fs, CPs and, of course, my mainstay nowadays, FPDs, and I still hold a reasonably sized portfolio including one property I have had since 1987.

As I look back over these forty years I realise that the biggest impact for me has not been the properties or the profit but the people; they've helped me and allowed me to develop but, more importantly, many of the people I've worked with and met over that time have become lifelong friends.

I originally trained as a chartered accountant and, although I completed all the training, passed all the exams and worked for the great and mighty Price Waterhouse, as it was then, I don't think accountancy ever floated my boat in the way that property investing has done.

Property ignited my business passion then and it continues to do so, and it has allowed me to live my life as I choose.

I have invested while still working a very grown-up and proper job as a Finance Director and CEO; as a young woman; as a mum with baby in tow and then as an entrepreneurial business owner.

And in the most recent past my properties enabled me to be with my husband as he was dying from an aggressive cancer. While I spent my entire time with him (because that's what he wanted and I was able, and very willing, to grant him that), the rental properties kept the wolf from the door, paid to feed the cats and kept our children in their various educational establishments.

Only a few weeks before he died I chucked £100k at an FPD with a group of friends, knowing that it would have to 'do' for my property investing for a year if that's all I could manage – it was, and it 'did' very well.

The properties saved me at a very difficult, personal time – they protected me and my family and paid for us while we dealt with an awful situation, and they also allowed me the freedom to be able to grieve for a year and get myself back together after he had gone.

Curiously, that year has also given me the perspective and motivation to write this book, and so this is also the parting gift from my husband to me, as his death provided the catalyst, the perspective and the spur to finally write this all down. In return, this is my final gift for him: a book that will evermore be in print and in the ether as a perpetual memory for my dearest Martin and our three wonderful children, Emma, Michael and Claudia, without whom nothing would ever have been possible – or worthwhile.

As for the property investing, I'm still going and I still have the passion to continue for a long time yet – after all, I've got to try and solve our housing crisis. I will continue to address our housing shortage and house people as best I can, even if it is slowly, one property at a time.

And I'm now back in full swing and you'll be able to see me at property networks, and in seminar rooms and conference halls up and down the country. If you do, please come and say hello – it'll be good to meet you.

In the meantime, I wish you, primarily, your good health and then also your wealth and personal happiness.

2016 POSTSCRIPT

Well, well, hasn't 2016 seen the shake-up of the buy-to-let industry? If you read any of the daily press or take the media at face value it would suggest that any buy-to-let investor is about to slit their wrists or change business immediately. And yet I personally don't know any one of my peers or colleagues who is leaving this arena, and I'm certainly not changing anything I do, so what are the issues?

The 3% Additional Stamp Duty

From the 1st April 2016, there is now an 'investors' rate' of stamp duty (Stamp Duty Land Tax: SDLT), which broadly adds a further 3% of stamp duty to any transaction over £40k for the purchase of any second and subsequent property.

And in fact the March 2016 budget went further than previously indicated and there is *no* exemption for properties purchased through a company or for purchases of fifteen or more properties in one go. So anyone who has set up a company to counteract this (and against the guidance from FF) now has a spare company that isn't required!

However, most professional investors accept that any additional stamp duty is generally only a cash flow issue as any money paid out on purchase is effectively refunded on sale as a cost of acquisition through the CGT calculation.

For example: a property is purchased for £200k, and is sold three years later for £250k, and after costs of improvement of £15k have been incurred. Sales costs are £5k.

On purchase the stamp duty will now be £7,500, being: 0% up to the first £40k and then 3% on the first £125k = £3,750. Then 5% (2% = 3% investor rate) on the remaining £75,000 = £3,750, which totals £7,500.

When the property is sold after three years the CGT calculation (very simply and before any allowances) is:

Sales proceeds	£250,000	
Less Costs:		
Purchase	£200,000	
Stamp Duty	£7,500	
Enhancements	£15,000	£222,500
		£27,500
Less: sales or realisation costs (say)		£5,000
Amount subject to CGT		**£22,500**

Any stamp duty paid on purchase is therefore 'recovered' on sale. This extra stamp duty needs to be factored into our standard evaluations on property purchase and included in our property strategies.

If the strategy is to generate capital and the property is being purchased as either a B&F or a CP, then the stamp duty needs to be included in the costs and is effectively only a temporary cash flow item which could, for example, be held on a 0% credit card for the length of time needed to complete the project.

If, however, the strategy is to generate income and the property is intended to be either a standard buy-to-let or an HMO, then the additional cost of the stamp duty should be evaluated and included within the standard Wash its Face calculations.

To return to our simple illustration above, if we assume that the property is being purchased as a buy-to-let and the rent to be generated is £1,250 per month, the standard Wash its Face calculation is:

Rent	£1,250
Mortgage:	
75% LTV on the £200k purchase (5%)	£625
The stamp duty £7.5k (5%)	£31
Management fee allowance (10%)	£125
Other operating expenses (10%)	£125
Net cash flow	**£344**

At this stage we now have the choice of just including the stamp duty cost in the calculation as above, *or* we could then add the stamp duty funding amount to the rent and increase the rent to £1,281, i.e. £1,250 + £31.

If we add the stamp duty funding cost to the rent in this way, then the effect of the additional 3% stamp duty is zero.

Conclusion

Professional investors in the main are not overly concerned by the additional 3% stamp duty on purchase because it is purely a cash flow challenge to be managed alongside the investment strategy, and if handled professionally will result in no additional cash outlay to the investor.

In most cases the extra cost of the stamp duty will be passed directly onto the tenant, and that makes sense. If for instance, the Chancellor increases petrol duty we, the consumer, know that we are going to pay more for our fuel at the pump. This 3% stamp duty is the same: it's an increase in 'duty' which will be passed straight to the customer, or the tenant in this case.

Clause 24

Clause 24 is the section in the Finance Bill 2015–2016 that limits tax relief to the basic rate for interest on loans taken to acquire buy-to-let and other investment properties.

The current proposal is that from April 2017 property rental profits will be computed without the deduction of interest payments. Then the effect of the interest payments will be calculated separately when a tax reduction is applied, which eventually reduces the effect of the tax relief on interest payments to basic rate tax levels.

The changes are phased in over three years starting from 6th April 2017, with the new rules applying to 25% of the relevant interest in the first year, 50% in the second and 75% in the third. They apply in full on all relevant interest payments from 6th April 2020.

However, there are several challenges to this proposal, including a significant legal challenge being mounted by a collection of investors and being made via the high legal profile of Cherie Blair's law firm.

The legal challenge appears to have some merit as it rests on the claim that the change flouts the long-established principle of taxation that expenses incurred wholly and exclusively for the purposes of business are deductible when calculating the taxable profits.

The legal view is widely supported by lawyers and accountants and hence must have some validity.

There was no obvious mention of this issue in the March 2016 budget and the government have at least a year to adjust their thinking and amend the proposal or even remove it.

Conclusion

Do nothing about this at the moment! But watch our website www.fieldingfinancial.com for news.

The European Credit Directive

The European Credit Directive ended its consultation period on 16th March 2016 and went live from Monday 21st March.

What is it about? It introduced the Mortgage Credit Directive (MCD) which is European legislation designed to bring the whole of Europe into line for mortgages with an intention to protect consumers. MCD will be implemented in the UK through rules set by the Financial Conduct Authority (FCA).

The main changes to mortgage lending resulting from the MCD are: some buy-to-let mortgages will become regulated by the FCA, and there will be a phased move to a Europe-wide standardised set of disclosure information to customers, via a European Standardised Information Sheet (ESIS).

In addition, lenders' sales processes and documentation will need to be reviewed for compliance and there will be two main implications from a conveyancing perspective:

- The MCD introduces a reflection period of at least seven days, which is to give the consumer time to compare offers and assess their implications. The reflection period will need to be incorporated into the conveyancing process.

- The MCD requires the credit agreement to be binding for this period.

Overall, as the UK is ahead of most other European countries in terms of its credit, there is less impact here with these types of changes than in other European countries, but one thing that will impact the UK is the introduction of:

Consumer Buy-to-Let (CBTL) Mortgages

Fundamentally a CBTL mortgage is borrowing for an amateur property investor, where the mortgage or remortgage is for a property that has been inherited or acquired with no specific purpose for it to be the owner's main or significant business. Illustrative examples given by one provider say:

- If a remortgage application is for a customer's only BTL property and they have previously resided in it as owner (e.g. Let to Buy), we will expect this to be treated as a CBTL application.

But:

- If a customer is purchasing a property with the sole intention of letting it out, we expect this to be considered a Business BTL application.

- If a customer already has other BTL properties we expect their application to be considered a Business BTL.

Therefore, as long as the borrower is acting as a professional then the normal investment mortgages will apply.

NB: CBTL mortgages will be regulated by the FCA and BBTL (Business Buy-to-Lets) will not.

And once again for clarity:

- Non-regulated BBTL is when a customer is deemed to be, or has identified themselves as, acting by way of a business in taking out a BTL mortgage.

- A BTL loan is on a property that has been bought for business purposes for the sole purpose of letting it out.

- If the borrower has never lived in it and has a portfolio of properties.

And:

- Lenders will require a signed declaration from the borrower to confirm the borrower is acting wholly for business purposes. Also, anyone associated with the transaction must have no reason to think this is incorrect.

Conclusion

Be professional, with a strategic business plan and an investor's qualification (which can be obtained at Fielding Financial of course!), and mortgages will be BBTL and no significant change will result for the professional property investor.

One final note – there is **NO** change expected to this legislation as a result of the BREXIT vote.

2016 POSTSCRIPT: SUMMARY

The government have an interesting dilemma here. On the one hand they need the professional, private landlords because the rate of houses that are owner occupied is dropping alongside a reduction in the availability and amount of socially provided housing. The professional landlords provide the accommodation that fills the gap and bridges the shortage between supply and demand for housing. That's a vital provision of a fundamental product in our society and our economy.

However, *if* private landlords are going to be providing so much of our society's housing needs, then the government needs to make sure that the housing is safe and that the people providing it are professional and adhere to professional standards of law and decency.

So the intention of the government is to scare off any amateur in this arena – and they're doing a great job with that! But they can't scare off the professional investor, otherwise too few houses will be available, social housing waiting lists will get even longer and many people will be without homes.

It's a fine balance and the government does appear to be supportive of the professional investor – and there are relatively few of us here; certainly less than 10% of all investors are what I call 'professional'. For instance, the government has given us development opportunities, so now under the permitted development rules we can convert offices and certain other commercial buildings into residential units without the need for planning permission. That is certainly an activity that most professionals would have in a strategy for a property business, and it helps create accommodation units and fulfil demand. That's a win-win strategy for the government *and* the professional investor, but it's unlikely to affect the amateur.

It is no surprise to me that they have labelled the new buy-to-let mortgage product the BBTL – because they want business owners to be in this arena and not just amateur investors with a property or two that they keep as a hobby.

In summary, then, the professional investor is accepting of the changes that are happening – I certainly feel that's it's about time we did something in this industry and I fully expect there to be full regulation, licencing, accreditation, qualification and a professional body for property investors in the near future. That sort of regime is not for the faint-hearted or the amateur, but it *is* right for the professional business owner who understands the property market and the crucial demand and supply issues.

And of course, if we do approach this professionally the returns are still way ahead of any other asset class or investment – so it's very much worth the effort!

ABOUT THE AUTHOR

Gill Fielding is a self-made millionaire with a no-nonsense, positive approach to finance and a personal mission to educate the nation in managing and improving their own financial position. She is best known for her appearance on Channel 4's *The Secret Millionaire* when she gave away nearly £250,000 to good causes.

Gill is a naturally gifted presenter who appears regularly on television and radio programmes. She has spoken in all five continents on macro economic affairs, wealth creation, financial education, investing skills as well as personal finance, motivational and inspirational topics.

As well as being a Secret Millionaire on Channel 4, she has been a Celebrity Egghead (BBC Two), a guest at the Hotel GB (Channel 4) and a business expert on *The Apprentice – You're Fired* (BBC Two). Gill is currently a financial expert for a regular show for BBC radio and has also contributed to ITN and Channel 4's election coverage. She also makes regular appearances as a financial commentator for the BBC, ITV and CNBC channels as well as appearing in many other TV shows around the world.

Gill co-founded and owns Fielding Financial which she set up in order to help anyone achieve what she describes as Financial Freedom. She has also written and presented a DVD entitled *Riches*, where she shares her Seven Secrets of Wealth which aims to help people transform their lives.

She is an eager supporter of many worthwhile causes and still supports all the families she met as part of the Secret Millionaire process as well as three national charities: Shelter, Mencap and Make a Wish. Gill is also a patron of Worthing and Adur Chamber of Commerce, and has been a Development Board member of RADA (with such luminaries as Duncan Bannatyne and Sir Richard Wilson).

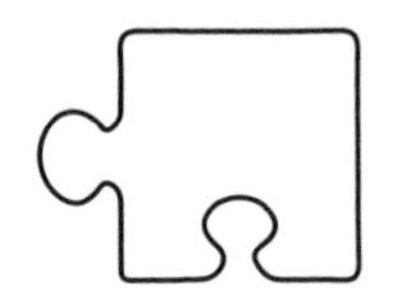

INDEX

NOTES

NOTES

NOTES

NOTES

NOTES

NOTES

NOTES

NOTES

NOTES

NOTES

NOTES